# *Money Matters*

# MONEY

*The Hassle-Free, Month-by-Month*

# MATTERS

*Guide to Money Management*

PAUL N. STRASSELS

WILLIAM B. MEAD

ADDISON-WESLEY PUBLISHING COMPANY, INC.

Reading, Massachusetts • Menlo Park, California
Don Mills, Ontario • Wokingham, England
Amsterdam • Bonn • Sydney • Singapore • Tokyo
Madrid • Bogotá • Santiago • San Juan

**Library of Congress Cataloging-in-Publication Data**

Strassels, Paul N.
  Money matters.

  Includes index.
  1. Finance, Personal.   I. Mead, William B.
II. Title.
HG179.S845   1986        332.024        86–10733
ISBN 0–201–07222–X

---

Text design by Outside Designs
Set in 10½ point Century Expanded by Compset, Inc., Beverly, Mass.

ABCDEFGHIJ-DO-89876

First printing, December, 1986

# *Contents*

## THE BASICS

## JANUARY: *Setting Up Shop*

## NOVEMBER: *Saving for Retirement*

## DECEMBER: *Staying "Rich"*

# Acknowledgments

We did not sit down one day to gather all the information for this book. We have been accumulating it for years, in connection with the articles, columns, books, and television scripts that we have written. This is an ongoing process, and we benefit continually from the wisdom and generosity of many knowledgeable professionals in such fields as taxes, investments, insurance, and credit. These allies are too numerous to name, but we thank them all.

We also thank the editors who have encouraged and improved our work. We are particularly indebted to the thirty-six city and regional magazines that subscribe to our monthly column. That column cements our partnership and provided the inspiration for this book. Bill is especially grateful to *The Washingtonian* and to editors Jack Limpert, Margaret Cheney, Ken DeCell, and Randy Rieland.

Thanks also, from both of us, to Anne Tuthill, Arnold and Elise Goodman, and Jim Wade.

# How to Use This Book

Everything in this book is designed to save you time, make you money, and help you meet your financial goals.

This book will show you how to make intelligent decisions on your own. We'll tell you just what to do and when to do it. We've divided the year into twelve themes, and we've broken the chores of money management into fifty-five lessons. Every lesson is geared to take full advantage of the new tax law. Our Monthly Planner tells you which lessons to use, month by month.

Our program is flexible, and you can jump in at any month of the year. We earmark January for the lessons that start you on your way, but you can as easily tackle those lessons in May or October or any other month. You don't have to accomplish every lesson in the next year; our advice will work whenever you choose to follow it. Feel free to shift themes from one month to another. We're giving you a system, but we're not trying to turn you into a robot. The only inflexible dates are those imposed by the Internal Revenue Service. They're noted in boldface on the Monthly Planner.

Some of our lessons are so short that you'll read and digest them in just a few minutes. Others are longer and require work on your part. Some lessons require your attention only once during the year; others cover topics that come up two or three times.

We've purposely designed a program that doesn't take a lot of time. We've done most of your financial shopping for you, and we give you toll-free telephone numbers and other quick keys to financial success. But you can't put your money on autopilot. On average, you'll need to commit an hour or two a week. Change the calendar if you wish, but don't ignore it. The calendar is a useful discipline. If you shortcut the system, you'll shortcut your own prospects.

This book is not for money hobbyists, and it is not for dreamers. Our system spares you the voluminous reading and ledger or computer work that financial moles enjoy. We offer you proven ways to make money on your investments, save money on your taxes, and otherwise handle your finances wisely and profitably. But we cannot make you rich quick. We offer no hot tips. We will not make you the most glamorous investor on the block, although you may become the most successful.

The only secret to successful money management is realizing that there are no secrets and knowing what you are doing and why. So we will guide you, but we will not make your decisions for you. We will never tell you to take a step blindly.

We will help you sort through the chaff. We will tell you why you can cheerfully ignore many investments that are touted in magazines and newspapers. We will help you concentrate on things that matter to you and put aside things that do not. We know that you want to make your money grow but don't want to spend a lot of time doing it. Money is *our* specialty, not yours. The more we work with it, the more we realize how simple and straightforward money can be, for those who understand it.

If you are married, this book is for both of you. One of our first lessons—number 5—is one of the most important: both of you depend on your money, so both of you should share in its care and growth.

If you follow our plan, you will have very little to do with stockbrokers, financial planners, and other salespeople. You don't need them. They need you. Stay out of their clutches. This book will show you how to make your own decisions, for your own benefit. Nearly all of the investments we recommend can be ordered by mail, with no sales commission tacked on.

In large part, this book is a shopper's guide. The financial field is a colorful and confusing bazaar, with a continual array of new products, each touted with its own razzmatazz. Unless you like to read prospectuses and good, gray journals like *Investor's Daily*, you can't evaluate all these wares.

That's our job. We've gone to the trouble of finding the best investments, the best insurers, the best credit cards, the best tax strategies, even a very few publications that you'll need from time to time. We've studied them and tested them, and we enthusiastically recommend them. Every one is simple and straightforward and easy to use. We have no financial or personal interest in anything that we recommend.

But there are professionals out there who do have a vested interest in selling you something. Our approach makes these professionals shudder. For example, in Lesson 40, we tell you how to find the very best life insurance policy by making one toll-free telephone call. Insurance sales reps will turn pale at the thought. In Lesson 27, we tell you how to find the very best yield on a certificate of deposit. The bank very likely will be hundreds of miles from your home, and your neighborhood bankers will throw up their hands in despair. In Lesson 25, we advise you to ignore options, commodities, warrants, and even individual stocks. To a stockbroker, that's treason.

This book is personal. We benefit from our differing perspectives, and we think you'll benefit, too. Both of us became familiar with personal money management through experience. Bill learned about investments from his grandfather, who was an active investor and managed the investments of a small foundation. Bill later wrote extensively for *Money* magazine, authoring thirteen cover stories and earning two prestigous journalism awards. He is now an associate editor of *The Washingtonian*. Paul spent five years with the Internal Revenue Service as a tax law specialist and for the last ten years has been writing and lecturing about taxes and family money management. His 1979 book *All You Need to Know about the IRS* was a best-seller, and his year-round series of tax and economic tips is televised nationwide. For the last four years, we have worked together on a syndicated magazine column, covering personal finance for the readers of thirty-six city and regional magazines.

Our book is not an encyclopedia. We don't pretend that our approach is the only approach. But it is a winning approach, tailored for you. With the help of this book, you will become a successful money manager within one year—and without sacrificing much of your precious spare time.

Turn to our Monthly Planner, starting with the current month. You can begin our plan any month of the year, but you should set aside your first month to accomplish "The Basics," Lessons 1–6. All our investment advice follows from this beginning. Keep all tax dates firmly in mind, as they are inflexible. Other than these two exceptions, you can readjust our timetable to suit your needs. Best wishes for a happy and prosperous future.

# THE BASICS

Successful money management is easy if you follow a few

logical steps.

# Keep It Simple

Nothing about money that really matters is terribly complicated. Simple steps that you understand will earn you more money, with less risk, than any of the "sophisticated" strategies touted by Wall Street.

To manage your money and make it grow, you need to watch what you spend, and you need to invest your savings so they'll meet your future needs. Keeping watch on your spending is hard; we all keep on waiting for that magic day when we pay all our bills and still have lots of money left over. But profitable investing is no longer difficult. Brokers and Wall Street hobbyists just make it look that way.

Years ago, the best investments and the best investment advice were reserved for wealthy insiders. But no longer. The financial markets have become democratized. Today, anyone with a little discretionary income can tap the same high yields, get the same high-powered advice, and buy the same investments as a Wall Street professional. And you can do it without paying much in fees or commissions.

To be sure, many of today's fashionable investments are dreadfully complicated. When you hear acquaintances talking about options or warrants or commodities futures, it's easy to feel like an ignoramus who's missed the boat. But those are high-risk investments. The vast majority of people who try them lose their money, including many pin-striped "professionals." Some people love to play the money game, just as others love to play roulette or blackjack. Let them. We prefer investments that are easier to understand, more likely to pay off in the long term, and demand less time and anxiety on our part. The new tax law enhances the value of these straightforward investments.

Plenty of them are available, including many that offer superb opportunities for growth. Indeed, the competition for your savings dollar is fierce, and many of the competitors have adopted the refreshing idea that the best way to attract your dollars is to give you a good return, without hassle or complication. The best investments, and the best savings strategies, are straightforward and provide clear choices that let you balance risk against reward, income today against a nest egg tomorrow, and taxable return against a return that may be less but is sheltered from income tax.

The same is true when it comes to insurance, tax-saving strategies, and other important elements of your financial life. The right choices are not obscure, but to find them you have to cut through the thickets of jargon and hot air and sales blarney that lead so many people astray. The lessons that follow will help you cut through these thickets and find the strategies and investments that fit your budget and your goals.

# *The Tools; or, Why Budgeting Your Time Is as Important as Budgeting Your Money*

To make a personal financial plan work, you must be willing to do a little thinking before you act. You must be willing to commit yourself to a certain amount of time on a regular basis, set goals for yourself, and review your progress.

An extremely successful friend of ours has a small wooden box on the corner of her desk. On the top of the box is engraved "To learn the secret of success, just open this box." When you lift the lid, you find a small slip of paper inside with two words written on it—"Hard work."

That holds true for successful money management. If you want to win the money game—and you can—you have to be willing to invest a certain amount of time and effort. We've found, over the years, that the investment needs to be systematic. An occasional hour here and a sporadic weekend there just doesn't work. Month in and month out you need to devote a few hours to your money on a regular schedule.

We're not talking about huge chunks of time. Nothing could be further from the mark. Actually, you can succeed in today's complex financial world if you devote as little as two hours a week or so to your money.

Make your commitment to succeed. Then grab your calendar and decide when you will sit down and pore over your finances. You'll need time at the beginning of each month to work on your budget. You'll need time to go over your taxes, investments, insurance, credit, and more. The way we have set up our program, you won't have to spend long hours at any one task.

Commitment is what you need. Not broken promises.

To begin, you should collect the tools you will require. You'll want a loose-leaf notebook so you can prepare your monthly budget and net worth statements. You'll want a small calculator. You may also want to find your last income tax return.

Some people get all excited and jump headfirst into planning their financial affairs, spending a great deal of money on fancy equipment. It's not necessary. You don't need expensive bound notebooks.

You also don't need a computer. We know that computers are the rage, and there are tons of programs promising to make personal finances easy. Don't believe it. People go out and buy a personal computer and sophisticated software programs, the price tag for which can amount to thousands of dollars. Then the computer sits idle because people don't use it to handle their money any more than they used to use paper and pencil.

Both of us use computers in our work and have become great fans of this technology. However, we feel that there is no need for you to invest in a home computer or buy a money management program simply to handle your finances. Our system works just fine with such inexpensive tools as paper, pencil, notebook, and calculator. If you want to use a computer to record your financial activity, go right ahead, but it's not necessary. We don't, even though we could.

To budget your time efficiently, we suggest that you set aside time at the beginning of each month. You might reserve one or two week nights right at the first of the month to work on your budget, write your checks, review your savings, and take care of the other items we suggest you review that particular month.

Once you have allotted your time for the entire year, you should then sit down quietly and thoughtfully and set out your financial goals. Record them on a piece of paper in the front of your notebook. Discuss them with your family if you have one. Keep them reasonable and attainable, but don't aim too low. We've found that articulating your goals is a step that too many people overlook. Without financial goals, you will just drift. Your finances will proceed, but not progress.

Some goals you may want to achieve are:

1. Meeting the college needs of your children.
2. Funding a comfortable retirement.

3. Saving to purchase a home.
4. Earning more on your investments than what the banks are paying.
5. Digging yourself out of debt.
6. Paying for a nice vacation rather than financing it.
7. Retiring at age sixty rather than sixty-five.
8. Providing for an aging parent.

All these are worthwhile, and all take money. Collecting that money doesn't happen by accident.

Once you identify your goals, separate them into long-term and short-term. For example, you might have a short-term goal of fully funding your retirement account this year. You might have a long-term goal of retiring with $1 million in the bank or financing your four-year-old son's college education.

With the tools collected and your long-term and short-term goals outlined, get started with the current month's financial planning.

But don't forget to periodically review and evaluate the progress you are making with your finances. We can talk all we want about your money plan, about how you can save and make more money, how you can invest more wisely, and how you can keep your money out of the hands of the Internal Revenue Service. But without evaluating your progress, none of this exercise works. Plans change. Some are successful, others are not. The unsuccessful ones need to be revised.

For example, let's consider retirement planning. You want a comfortable retirement, and that's not going to happen by accident. You need to salt away a certain amount every year to supplement Social Security and a pension from your employer, assuming you are eligible for one. You can evaluate your progress against your plan to see that you are meeting your savings goal each year. In addition, your retirement savings need to earn a certain return that will enable you to reach your goal. If your retirement account has been earning 10 percent over the past few years when savings rates were high and that's what you have factored into your long-range plan, you may have to reevaluate now that yields have declined. An alternative is to move your account into investments that are earning a higher rate of return.

Planning your goals and reevaluating them should be done at least once each year. January is a good time. However, if you start this book in October, for example, you should sit down then to set out your goals. That way, you will be able to track your progress in the months and years ahead.

## *Run Your Own Show*

Don't let other people decide your future. Make your own decisions, and remember that brokers, insurance agents, and other sales reps push the products that earn them the highest commissions.

Within all of us, even those who reek of self-assured wealth, lurk two conflicting desires. We would like to get richer, and we would like to have some Big Daddy or Big Mommy show us the way. Lots of people set themselves up as Big Daddys or Big Mommys. They are friendly and likable, and they talk with an assurance that is hard to resist. Gee, you think. Anyone who talks that positively must *really know.*

These are salespeople. They may call themselves agents or brokers or financial advisers, but their business is selling stocks or bonds or insurance policies or simply advice to people like you. They are not evil; sales is an honored occupation in our society. Some of them can be quite helpful. But they have their own desires. They would like to get richer, and the money that they want is yours. Keep your hand on your wallet. Getting rich is not that easy.

Sure, you need advice; we all do. But it is one thing to consider advice and quite another to fall into the common trap of going with someone else's decisions. You—and your spouse, if you're married—are your own best expert. No one else knows as much about you or cares as much, and no one else will have to live with the decisions that are made about your finances, good or bad.

Don't think you're immune to the Big Daddy syndrome. We're not. Bill can still remember (ouch!) selling a favorite stock at $19, on the advice of a veteran broker and a prominent portfolio manager, both of whom confidently predicted that it was on its way down. (It closed the other day at $63.50.) We hope we've learned from our mistakes. We'll surely make more, but at least they'll be our own.

Money is at once the most practical and most emotional of subjects, and it is hard to stay objective. What's more, there are no certainties about money, and all of us are looking for certainty. If you doubt that otherwise intelligent and successful people almost beg to place their financial affairs in the hands of others, listen to these three professionals, all of whom hold jobs in the Washington, D.C., area, where we live and work.

- Theodore Bahr, broker and financial planner for IDS Financial Services: "I have people coming into my office who don't understand the lingo and don't want to understand. Financial planning should educate you, so you're in a position to make intelligent decisions."
- Mary Malgoire, president of Malgoire Drucker, Inc., a financial-planning firm: "People have this idea that if they go to a financial adviser, he'll make them rich. That is such a terrible, terrible misconception. What I can do is separate out the emotion and give them information that will help them make the right decisions."
- Leslie J. Silverstone, senior vice president for Dean Witter, one of the nation's largest brokerage firms: "Too many people want to just put their money in the hands of a broker and go to sleep. They want to be sold. People have to take some responsibility on their own."

Although it is no secret that brokers are sales reps, not investment analysts, those who practice the trade are continually surprised by the open gullibility of customers, many of whom are resounding successes in law, medicine, business, and other fields.

Silverstone offers this analogy: He went shopping for a first-class radio, one that would bring in shortwave transmissions. He could have read up on radios, but instead he went to a store and looked for a salesperson who appeared to be knowledgeable. "I didn't want to read a catalog describing six radios," he says. "I wanted to be sold. That's the way people are with money. They want that hard sell. So the good salesman is going to do a land-office business, even though he may not be the best investment adviser. Most people don't want to work with somebody who's honest and conservative, and maybe talks a little slow."

Part of that desire, Silverstone says, is the yearning we all share for someone who really knows what's around the corner and who can tell us how to cash in. Take interest rates, which affect stock and bond prices; Silverstone says he's asked about the future course of interest rates not by one or two people a day, but by dozens. He replies ambivalently. Many other brokers would give a positive response—after all, the customer asked—and make a sale.

That is not to say that brokers and other investment seers are fakes; most of them believe their own predictions. The executive committee of one of New York's biggest banks used to meet once a week and share an important ritual: each member would write on a slip of paper his or her prediction of interest-rate trends for the week to come, and these jottings would be averaged into a forecast. Trouble is, the forecasts were wrong as often as they were right, just as your forecast or ours would be. The meetings tended to remind the bankers of their own continuing fallibility, so they dropped the ritual.

The plain truth is that no one, not even Paul Volcker or T. Boone Pickens, can predict the future of interest rates, the stock market, bond prices, real estate values, or the gross national product.

Another basic truth is that salespeople make bigger commissions on some products than on others, and their evaluations and forecasts tend to fit their pocketbooks. Most brokers, for example, make more by selling you a long-term bond trust, one that matures in twenty or thirty years, than by selling you a short-term bond trust that matures in about ten years. Surprise! Most brokers recommend long-term trusts, even though the ten-year trusts are safer.

Insurance agents, too, make much larger commissions by selling you policies that build up cash value—a category that includes whole life, universal life, and a few other variations. Virtually every objective observer recommends simple, inexpensive term life insurance, but agents don't make much money selling term life. They don't recommend it, either; they recommend whole life and universal life.

The most obvious and eager advisers—or Big Daddys—are full-service stockbrokers, who charge for their advice by imposing higher commissions than discount brokers. On a small transaction, full-service brokers may charge just a little more than discounters; on a large transaction, they may charge twice as much, or even more. Yet only 3 to 5 percent of the commission money received by full-service brokers is spent on securities research, and most independent observers do not greatly admire the research that brokerage houses churn out.

Mark Hulbert edits *The Hulbert Financial Digest*, a monthly newsletter that compares other investment newsletters by statistically tracking the performance of the portfolios they recommend. (*Hulbert Financial Digest*, 643 South Carolina Ave. S.E., Washington, D.C. 20003.) Hulbert would like to track the recommendations of Merrill Lynch, Dean Witter, E. F. Hutton, and other major brokerage houses but says they have declined to cooperate. "If their recommendations were beating the market, we'd be hearing from them," Hulbert says.

A few brokers publish performance reports on their own recommendations, including Dean Witter, Prudential-Bache, and Shearson Lehman/American Express. Hulbert is not impressed. "I have a skeptical attitude about any in-house report of their record," he says. "For one thing, how many other clients are getting their recommendations before you are?"

He's right. As an individual client, you're not likely to be at the top of a brokerage firm's call list. First in line are pension funds and other institutional investors, who trade millions of dollars at a time. By the time a recommendation has worked its way to the broker on your account, and your broker has reached you, the stock may have tacked on several points as a result of purchases by clients who were given the recommendation first. When you buy, they may be selling—and pocketing that quick profit.

Besides, not all brokers' recommendations are unbiased. Most brokerage firms double as investment bankers and underwriters. When a broker calls you to recommend a particular stock, it's quite possible that her brokerage firm has taken on a big block of that stock as an underwriter or agent. The brokers, like soldiers down the line, have been ordered to unload that stock and probably have been offered fat commissions. You, and thousands of other similar individual customers, are like turkeys in a turkey shoot.

That's not all. Suppose a brokerage firm you worked for had General Motors as a valued client and your job was to analyze auto stocks. Would you feel free to publish a negative report about GM stock?

Negative reports aren't popular in brokerage houses, anyway. "They publish a far greater preponderance of 'buy' signals than 'sell' signals," says Hulbert. "Right before Continental Illinois Bank went down, about the worst recommendation on it from any major brokerage house was a 'hold.' "

The biggest drawback, of course, is that a broker gets paid when you trade, whether you are buying or selling and whether you are making money or losing money. If a broker had told his clients twenty years ago to buy IBM and hold on to it, the clients would have prospered and the broker would have starved. "I know many fine brokers," says Robert E. Torray, president of Torray Clark & Co., a firm that manages billions of dollars in pension-fund assets. "But there's a big conflict of interest in that business, and it's almost impossible to overcome."

Nevertheless, brokerage firms know that investors are looking for an expert, and they dress their salespeople accordingly, with lots of status and class. Surely, a vice president wouldn't be just a salesperson! Oh, yes she would. One Merrill Lynch office in downtown Washington has twenty vice presidents, and you can be sure that their job is selling securities, not running the company. After all, Merrill Lynch is headquartered in New York. A broker can have the sleaziest of reputations among his colleagues, but if he produces a lot of business, his firm will give him a big title and set him up in an impressive office, and competitors will try to hire him away with six-figure bonuses.

The best brokers—that is, the ones who are the most productive—make more than a million dollars a year in commissions. Remember that next time you catch yourself thinking, Aw, shucks, Sally is just making an honest living off little investors like me.

You can use a broker as a sounding board to make sure your own decisions aren't skewed by your emotions. "If a broker does nothing more for you than make you establish ground rules and stick with them, that's enough," says Les Silverstone. Mary Malgoire makes the same case for using a financial planner: "It gets you more organized, more disciplined about your money. It's like using a teacher to learn to play the piano; you wouldn't practice if you didn't take the lessons."

Fair enough. But never forget that only one person is thoroughly dedicated to your interests. That's you. By reading this book and letting it be your financial planner, you'll use proven, straightforward, time-saving strategies, and you'll find that you can manage your own affairs surprisingly well. You may make a mistake or two (so do the professionals), but you'll gain self-confidence, save time for more pleasurable pursuits, and become increasingly prosperous. What's more, you'll sleep at night.

# LESSON 4

## The Wall Street Journal *and*
## *Other Publications You Can*
## *Cheerfully Ignore*

Daily financial news is for people who enjoy it or need it at work or want something to worry about. A consistent strategy works better than one that zigs and zags with turns in the news.

If financial publications bore you, our reading list would put you to sleep. We read, or at least scan, *The Wall Street Journal, Money* magazine, *Changing Times, Forbes, U.S. News & World Report, Boardroom Reports*, the "Money" section of *USA Today*, and the business section of the Sunday *New York Times*. For specialized reading on investments, we take *The American Association of Individual Investors Journal, Switch Fund Advisory, Schabacker's Mutual Fund Quarterly Performance Review*, the *Lipper Mutual Fund Performance Analysis, Standard & Poor's Outlook, The Professional Tape Reader, Jumbo Rate News*, and *Tiered Rate Watch*. To keep up with taxes, we read *Commerce Clearing House, Research Institute Reports*, and more.

We have to. We write about personal finance for a living. It's our job to weed through all this material and point you toward strategies that will work, without voluminous reading on your part. If you want to handle your financial chores in just a few hours a month, you can't take on the *Journal*, much less the dozens of other fine financial publications.

In truth, a smattering of financial reading can do as much harm as good. It's hard to stick with a simple, straightforward, and consistent strategy while continuously reading about newer and more glamorous alternatives. But a straightforward and consistent strategy is far superior to one that changes because of something new or because of some warning or forecast.

Not that you should stick your head in the sand. We assume you'll take note of important economic news, just as you take note of important international news. For example, you're certainly aware of the new Tax Reform Act. But your investment program will not benefit from the comments of Wall Streeters quoted in the daily stock-market stories. And the last thing you need to buy is Wall Street's latest creation, which was created to attract gullible investors.

*Money* and *Changing Times* are excellent magazines, aimed at prudent and ambitious investors and consumers. If you want to read them and have time, do so. You'll learn a lot. After a year or so, you'll probably note that the material tends to be repetitious. The publishers have to bring out a new issue every month, and there's only so much to be said about tax deductions, mutual funds, life insurance, and so forth. So the editors and writers find different ways to say the same things.

We conceived this book as a digest—a thorough and specific program for the thousands of Americans who want to use and invest their money wisely, without making a hobby or fetish of it and without exposing themselves to risky strategies. That doesn't mean you get by with no reading at all. As you read the lessons that follow, you'll find that we do occasionally recommend a booklet or a magazine or a newsletter. We call it our "Very Short Reading List." Here it is:

- To keep your money in the very best mutual funds, the annual mutual funds issue of *Forbes*, published in August or September, and one issue a year of *Schabacker's Mutual Fund Quarterly Performance Review*. (See Lesson 21 for address.)
- To get the highest yields on certificates of deposit, *Tiered Rate Watch*. (See Lesson 27 for address.)
- To get the most in financial aid for college, *Don't Miss Out: The Ambitious Student's Guide to Financial Aid*. (See Lesson 38 for address.)
- To help you save on taxes, *IRS Publication 17: Your Federal Income Tax*, free from the Internal Revenue Service. You can order this publication from the Internal Revenue Service Forms Distribution Center for your state.
- And this book.

# LESSON 5

## *No More Chauvinism; or, Why You and Your Spouse Should Handle Finances Together*

Financial planning needn't be a lonely and tedious chore, not when you can enlist the aid of a willing partner. In addition, it's not fair for one person to shoulder all of the responsibility for a family's financial well-being. Nor is it fair for one family member to be in the dark about the family's money. It's financially dangerous for one person to be in complete control of the purse strings. This lesson is intended to help single individuals (each represents a family unit) as well as married couples, although singles may find it uncomfortable at first to share the details of their financial lives with others.

Essentially, our message is this: financial planning is more than a one-person job. No one can do it all. You need to plan a month-by-month budget; purchase health, auto, life, and disability insurance coverages; prepare your taxes; stay up on your investments; and so on. All this has to be done in a constantly shifting financial environment. So how can you keep up? Our suggestion is to enlist the aid of a partner. Make it someone you can trust, a person who has your financial well-being at heart. If you're married, make it your spouse. If you're single, work with a trusted relative or close friend.

Don't be surprised if he or she does not want to be included in the family's financial-planning sessions. Finances can be tedious and sometimes even frightening to the person who has never had to participate before. Be insistent. Don't take no for an answer.

Here are four reasons we feel it is necessary for you to have a partner in handling your financial affairs:

1. It's a tough job. People are, by and large, earning more than ever before, especially married couples who both work outside the home. It's difficult to know everything about every aspect of finances today. There are many opportunities to make money—and to lose it. This may sound obvious, but when only one individual handles the family finances, the entire burden rests on that person's shoulders. A team approach works so much better. It's safer; one may offer suggestions, and ask questions, that the other hadn't even considered. Togetherness will expand your financial horizons.
2. It's a tedious job. It's not fair for one party to shoulder the entire burden, acting as a financial guru. Resentment often creeps in: the guru resents doing all the work while the other does nothing; the other person, in turn, resents being left out of the financial picture. A joint effort means that both of you will attend to the details of balancing the checkbook, working on a budget, and preparing tax returns.
3. It can bring you closer together and perhaps prevent some arguments. Too many families fight about money, or the lack of it. Could the reason for this be that only one is informed about the family's money dealings while the other is not? It's difficult to tell someone that a new refrigerator or lawn mower can't be afforded because the money has to go into a retirement account or that you can't go on a vacation because the money has to go into a child's education fund or to pay insurance premiums or to fund an annuity for an aging parent. Not only is it difficult to tell someone these things, it's also painful to hear them. When both work together, both know about these money constraints.
4. It's protection. If you have a reluctant partner who refuses to get involved with the finances, this argument is compelling.

It's an unfortunate fact that married couples separate, they divorce, or one partner dies prematurely. When that happens, the remaining partner is often left without a clue about financial matters.

Yet when both participate in the family's financial affairs while the marriage is intact, the often devastating results of a death or divorce are avoided.

Single individuals who do not discuss financial information with their parents and their brothers and sisters can find themselves facing financial dilemmas when there is a death or divorce in the family.

Let's talk about the special situation faced by single individuals. Where can they find someone to share in their financial-planning burdens and decisions? Singles may include those in their midtwenties fresh out of school, career people who have never married, divorced men and women who are still working, and retirees who either have never married or have lost a spouse.

Though you don't have a spouse, chances are that you do have some family. It may be a parent, brother or sister, son or daughter. Maybe there's an aunt, uncle, nephew, or niece that you're fond of and trust. If you aren't close to anyone in your family, you may find a friend in similar financial circumstances. You can work together on your finances. Even if you handle your money close to the vest, you should inform someone of what it is you're doing. At least write this information down and leave it with your attorney or banker. Chances are you have life insurance, a will, investments, and other assets that will need to be disposed of in the event of your death. Someone needs to know about your finances, even if not sharing in your day-to-day financial plan.

Here's how you can begin easing the load.

Together, or alone if you are single, develop your budget (see Lesson 8) and net worth statement (see Lesson 7). These tasks will take only half the time when you share them and will serve to inform both partners of the family's financial position.

Hold monthly budget sessions as indicated in the calendar we have presented. They will take only an hour or two.

Prepare your taxes—together. When married couples file joint returns, they pay taxes at lower rates than do single individuals. Since both husband and wife are required to sign a joint tax return, both should be equally aware of what's on it. If you qualify for a refund, both share in it. If you owe, the family will have to pay, and that affects both of you.

Tax-return preparation can be drudgery, especially the part that requires someone to collect and organize all your papers, records, and receipts for the past year. Put two on the job, and it can be accomplished in half the time.

Same goes for filling out the actual forms. While working together won't make the job any more fun, at least it will make things much easier. Also, there's less chance of overlooking a deduction or making an error in your calculations. For more on preparing your taxes, see Lesson 11.

Review employee fringe benefit plans together. This is particularly important when both husband and wife work. Both may be offered life and health plans from their respective employers, along with other benefits. Choose the most comprehensive benefits at the least cost to the family when you have the opportunity.

Check through your life, health, disability, auto, and homeowner's insurance policies. Again, make it a joint effort. If there is ever a problem, it is vital that both know where all the policy records are kept.

Pay your bills together. This miserable task is one that should be shared. No one enjoys doing it, so do it together. Maybe you'll decide that one of you should write the checks one month with the other doing the honors the following month. Together you can decide which accounts the money is to come from. It's not unusual for families to have joint and separate checking, savings, and investment accounts. Whatever division of salary and other income works best for you is fine. The point is that when you handle the bill paying together, both of you will be fully informed of the day-to-day operations of the family's finances.

Investment decisions should be made by the two of you. Don't let one of you be accused by the other of making poor investment decisions. Here's what happened to one friend of ours. It seems that his wife had inherited some stock from her father's estate twenty years ago. In that time, it had done nothing. The dividend was right around 2 percent, and in all that time, growth was almost nil. But because it had come from her father, she adamantly refused to sell. Finally, he convinced her to unload the dog of a stock; with her consent, he took the money and invested it in a blue-chip issue that was returning an 8 percent dividend plus enjoying better-than-average growth. It looked like a good move, resulting in more income and growth.

Then six months later, the original company was the target of a takeover. The value of its stock almost doubled in a month. And she was furious.

This illustrates why neither the husband nor the wife should be solely in charge of the investment decisions for the family and why a single individual should seek some help when thinking about investments. The entire family wins or loses depending on where and how the family's money is invested. It's not right to blame one person when an investment sours or to give undeserved credit when an investment takes off. It's a team effort.

We've heard the excuse too often that one person in the family has a head for finances while the other excels in other areas. That's rubbish. Both spend the family's money. Both want nice things.

Both need retirement accounts, auto insurance, savings, and budgets. Both must participate in the job of family financial planning.

Men don't handle finances any better or any worse than women. If spouses don't share the family's money dealings, they are only hurting themselves and their families. Don't be chauvinistic; there's no place for it here. Money plays no favorites. It's a much easier game to win when you have a partner with whom you can share the duties and responsibilities. You don't want to do it alone, and you shouldn't have to.

# *The Real Value of a Working Spouse, and Other Surprises*

More than half of all married couples find both husband and wife working outside the home. Together they make a lot of money, but a sizable chunk of it is eaten up in taxes, child care, extra transportation, and other costs. The amount of cash available to the family after taxes and expenses is often much less than you might think. If you are married, here's how to determine if that second job is financially worth the effort. If you're single and thinking of getting married sometime in the future, consider the net tax effect when two incomes are combined.

Working couples have become the rule rather than the exception. Statistically, working couples spend a larger percentage of their income on luxury and leisure than do couples with only one working spouse. Yet when asked why they work, the response is usually that the second salary allows the family to meet the everyday expenses of housing, food, transportation, and clothing.

Granted, the second salary means all these things and more— more savings, more trips, more financial peace of mind. However, it also means more expenses—expenses that the family would not have if that second wage earner opted to stay at home or perform social or volunteer work.

The expense that hits hardest is taxes, despite the cut in tax rates guaranteed by the 1986 Tax Reform Act. This includes both federal and state income taxes and Social Security taxes. And there are other expenses that are not far behind, such as an extra car, insurance costs, meals out, housekeeping, and child care, to name just a few.

Let's focus strictly on taxes for a minute. Once the government collects the extra federal income tax and Social Security taxes from the second salary, its value is not worth nearly as much as you might at first think. Take a look at the accompanying table. It shows the real value of the second salary when you add it to the first, after you pay federal income and Social Security taxes on it. We are assuming a married couple files a joint return, claims typical itemized deductions, and has one child. We used 1986 tax rates.

THE TRUE VALUE OF A SECOND SALARY

| If the first salary is: | $25,000 | $35,000 | $40,000 | $50,000 |
|---|---|---|---|---|
| A second salary of $15,000 equals: | $12,253 | $12,015 | $11,605 | $11,560 |
| 25,000 | 19,813 | 18,960 | 18,697 | 18,047 |
| 30,000 | 23,120 | 22,415 | 21,987 | 21,131 |
| 40,000 | 30,213 | 28,902 | 28,269 | 27,300 |

Take the example of a family with a single income amounting to $40,000. The at-home spouse is thinking about rejoining the work force. The question: Is it worth the effort to take a job paying $15,000, or should he or she hold out for a better-paying position or go back to school and try to improve skills? You decide. When piled on top of the $40,000 earned by the other spouse, that $15,000 really only amounts to $11,605, taking the extra federal income and Social Security taxes into account. That's less than $1,000 a month.

State and local income taxes will then take an additional percentage.

The 1986 Tax Reform Act changes the equation somewhat for that second income. Tax rates are cut substantially, first in 1987 and then again in 1988. In 1988 and later years, there are only two tax brackets, 15 percent and 28 percent, so the compounding effect of one income piled atop the other is not what it was in 1986.

You might think initially that the value of a working spouse has increased because of the latest tax law changes. Perhaps it has, once you take the lower individual tax rates, larger personal exemptions, and other modifications into account. But by all accounts any benefit will be slight. That's because the overall effect of the tax law change is to be revenue neutral. While your federal income taxes may indeed drop, state and local income taxes may increase. Deductions for IRAs, two-earner couples, income averaging, medical expenses, and consumer interest to name just a few are either repealed or substantially modified, counteracting the benefits of the tax rate reduction. Social security taxes are going nowhere but up.

Social Security taxes are unforgiving. Everyone pays. It's the closest thing we have to a pure tax. For 1986, the first $42,000 of an individual's wages was subject to Social Security tax, at a rate of 7.15 percent. The first wage earner, making $40,000 a year, paid $2,860 in Social Security. The second wage earner, making $15,000, paid $1,072.50. If that $15,000 additional income could have been earned by the first wage earner, only $2,000 of it would have been subject to Social Security; the remaining $13,000 would not. That would mean a tax savings of $929.50. Instead, it's a $929.50 tax bite.

For 1987, Social Security taxes will be even higher.

But that's just the tax situation. There's much more that goes into the equation of whether the salary offered for a particular second job is sufficient to justify it. The cost of commuting varies in different parts of the country. The cost of work clothing is probably higher in cold-weather areas than in the southwest. Child-care charges are higher in the cities than in small towns.

Although it is difficult to quantify such items, you should nevertheless attempt to come up with a ballpark dollar figure for each expense you might have to cover and then analyze your various options. For example, take commuting costs. If you use public transportation, that can amount to $4 a day or more. Multiply that by 240 workdays a year, and your out-of-pocket cost is $960.

If you join a car pool, your expenses may be less.

If you buy a second car that wouldn't otherwise be needed, you will be putting out a couple of thousand dollars a year. In addition, you will increase your auto insurance premiums. In some areas, you may have to pay extra taxes on the value of the automobile. Add to that the cost of parking, if you'll be working downtown. That can run another $5 a day or more, depending on where you live. And while the price of gas is down from what it was a few years ago, it will still be a sizable expense over the year.

You will pay extra for convenience. With both husband and wife working, the family will tend to eat fast foods more often. You may use the dry cleaner more, and you may hire someone to help with the housework and yardwork from time to time or even on a regular basis.

A major expense for working couples can be the cost of child care. This can amount to thousands of dollars a year for after-school care, day-care centers, and summer camp.

There are several tax benefits available to families where both the husband and wife work, although not as many as before tax reform.

The child- and dependent-care tax credit can help ease the strain of child-care costs. For those earning an income of more than $28,000, you can claim a tax credit up to 20 percent of what you spend on child care, with a maximum expense of $2,400 for one child and $4,800 for two or more. That means you can reduce your taxes by as much as $480 for one child and $960 for two or more. For those earning less than $28,000 a year, the credit increases as the income decreases, with the credit being increased by 1 percentage point for each $2,000 increment below the $28,000 level. The maximum child-care credit is 30 percent.

You can package your fringe benefits to best suit your family. You can take the most comprehensive health package offered from one employer and a disability plan from another. You should definitely take advantage of the full range of retirement programs offered by the two employers.

Your Individual Retirement Account (IRA) contributions can amount to $4,000. That's $2,000 per worker. When only one works, the maximum IRA contribution is $2,250 for the two of you. That's assuming neither of you is covered by a company retirement plan, or your family income is under $40,000. (See Lesson 50 for more details.)

Prior to recent tax law changes, a working couple was allowed to deduct 10 percent of the smaller salary, up to a maximum of $3,000. That generous tax break was called the two-earner deduction, and substantially benefited those who were in the highest income brackets. For example, if your combined income in 1986 was in the 45 percent tax bracket, that $3,000 deduction meant a $1,350 tax savings. The deduction was repealed as of January 1, 1987.

An alternative to accepting a job outside the home is to bring the job into the home. If you are in business for yourself, consider hiring your spouse rather than having him or her work for someone else. There are numerous tax advantages to this strategy. For example, if yours is an unincorporated business, salary paid to your spouse is not subject to Social Security taxes. That's a definite savings.

Another possibility is to start your own at-home business based on an activity that had hitherto been a hobby rather than accepting a job from someone else.


Certainly, there are many factors to take into consideration when an at-home spouse thinks about rejoining the work force, with financial considerations being only one. You must consider such intangibles as pride and personal growth, being home when the kids finish the school day, and the possibility of sending them to the finest colleges.

When it comes to a pure money decision, though, taxes play a major role, as do the various other expenses you will have. Based on your personal circumstances and views, tax rates, and the various deductions and credits you may avail yourself of, decide if it is worth the time and effort to work for the money being offered.

# JANUARY

## *Setting Up Shop*

You can't manage your money without knowing how much you have, how much you owe, and how much you spend. Whatever month you begin our program, you should <u>first</u> <u>figure your net worth</u> and <u>prepare a budget</u> before taking another step. <u>Update your budget monthly</u>; it's easy once you've started.

 *To Do*

- Fourth and final estimated tax payment due January 15
- Figure your net worth following form on pages 30 and 31
- If you have a family, develop a family security statement (see page 33)
- Create a month-by-month budget following form on page 39
  - If you can reconstruct your expenses for previous 12 months, do so; if not, go as far back as you can.
  - Compare your new budget estimates with reconstructed previous months

- Undertake preliminary tax planning session (see page 40)
- If you are making IRA contributions, do so this month if possible. See lesson 50, page 215 for the advantages of investing early in an IRA.

# *Figuring Your Net Worth*

Before you can decide what it is you want to accomplish with a financial plan, you need to determine your present state of affairs. That means you must determine your starting point. That's known as your net worth. You may be elated or terribly disappointed by the results of this exercise, but at least you will know where to begin your financial planning. And once you know your net worth, develop a family security statement. That's how you can determine whether your family would be able to manage financially in case of your untimely death.

It's important that you view your financial affairs in two parts. There are the day-to-day and month-to-month budgetary matters you need to be aware of, such as paying the bills, fixing the car, buying groceries. Take a look at Lesson 8 for the details of what's involved.

The other part of financial planning is long-term: where do you want your finances to be in five, ten, or even fifteen years? To craft a long-term financial plan, you need a starting point. You find it by determining your net worth.

Net worth is a simple concept. It involves nothing more than adding all your assets and subtracting the total amount of your liabilities. The result is your net worth.

However, this calculation is much easier said than done. In fact, too few people bother to compute their net worth, and yet it is something you should do once a year.

We recommend that you go to the trouble each January. The timing is ideal. However, if you pick up this book in midyear, we urge you to work up a net worth statement immediately rather than wait until next January. It's that important.

You can obtain preprinted net worth forms from your local banker, or you can develop your own on a blank sheet of paper.

## NET WORTH
as of (month, date, year)

*Assets*

Cash on hand

Checking account  No. 1 _____

      No. 2 _____

      No. 3 _____

Savings account  No. 1 _____

      No. 2 _____

      No. 3 _____

Money market fund _____

Cash management account _____

Certificate of deposit  No. 1 _____

      No. 2 _____

      No. 3 _____

Investments (cost and value as of 12/31):

 Stocks  No. 1 _____

    No. 2 _____

    No. 3 _____

    No. 4 _____

    No. 5 _____

    No. 6 _____

 Mutual fund  No. 1 _____

     No. 2 _____

     No. 3 _____

     No. 4 _____

 Real estate (estimated fair market value as of 12/31)

  Personal residence _____

  Other real estate _____

Pensions

 IRA  No. 1 _____

   No. 2 _____

 Keogh _____

 Vested company benefits _____

 Annuities _____

Personal items (jewelry, furniture) _____

Automobile  No. 1 _____

     No. 2 _____

Cash value of whole life insurance _____

Debts owed to you by others  No. 1 _____

         No. 2 _____

Interest in estate or trust _____

Interest in business ventures _____

Other assets _____

   TOTAL ASSETS _____

*Liabilities*
Home mortgage
Other real estate loans
Auto loan  No. 1
        No. 2
Bank loan  No. 1
        No. 2
Outstanding credit card balances
Installment loans
Balance on life insurance loan
Debts owed to others
    TOTAL LIABILITIES

Assets (from previous page) minus liabilities equals your current net worth. Save this statement.

Just follow the sample we provide. It's not difficult. Lenders typically have the forms on hand because anytime you want to take out a loan, you will be asked to prepare a net worth statement on yourself.

Here's how to go about preparing a net worth statement.

The first thing you should do is write at the top of the statement "Net Worth as of (whichever date you start)."

Then begin listing your assets. The first items to write down are the amount of cash you have on hand as well as what's in your checking and savings accounts. That's relatively easy to determine.

Then list other cash accounts you may have, such as money market mutual funds, cash management accounts, and certificates of deposit.

Go on to your investment portfolio. List the market value of your investments as of the date of your statement. Your brokerage reports should be a valuable source of information here.

Your investments may include real estate. Note the fair market value of the property. The mortgages will be taken care of in the liabilities section of the form.

Record the current value of pension rights you have accumulated. This may include Individual Retirement Accounts (IRAs), Keoghs, and vested company pension benefits. If you are vested, you have the right to the funds even if you should leave the firm.

It's difficult, but try to estimate as best you can the value of your household furnishings and jewelry. Don't write down what you paid or what it would cost to replace the items but rather what you would get if you tried to sell.

Note the trade-in value of your car (or cars). Again, ignore anything you owe on the vehicle. Car loans will be recorded later as a liability.

If you own life insurance that has a cash value, record that amount here.

Do the same for annuities, the one-time investments you make where the return is paid to you on retirement.

If anyone owes you a debt, note the outstanding amount.

If you have a financial interest under a will, trust, or estate, write down what it's worth.

However, do not count on money that is not absolutely guaranteed. Do not include future wages, salaries, fees, or commissions you anticipate receiving. If you will receive a sum of money under an irrevocable trust when you reach a certain age, then by all means put that down. But if you simply anticipate that you will inherit some cash under the will of a person who is still living, don't add that into your net worth statement. If it's not a certainty, don't count on the money.

One item that is particularly difficult to value is a small business you own. You have to determine what that firm would be worth if you were no longer there to operate it. It may be worth nothing more than the value of the equipment you own. That's particularly true for service enterprises. However, don't sell yourself short. Your client list may have value even without you. The company may be sold for cash. It may have accumulated cash in the bank. All these are assets you should be aware of.

You may have a partnership business interest with others. Again, note the current value.

Make a note of anything else that you own of value.

Then total your assets.

Next address your liabilities.

Liabilities come in all sizes and shapes. Be complete as you record what you owe to others on this side of your net worth statement. Include loans you owe, outstanding tax bills, business debts, and the like.

Start by writing down the amount of the mortgage loans you still owe as of the first of the year.

Do the same for your car loans and outstanding balances on credit cards.

If you've borrowed against life insurance policies, record those loans, too.

If you have borrowed from a bank, savings and loan, credit union, or private individual or firm, put down the outstanding balances.

Don't include recurring household responsibilities in this list. You shouldn't add in utility bills, groceries and the cleaners here, just outstanding bills that are paid over a period of time.

Your net worth is the difference between what you own (your assets) and what you owe to others (your liabilities).

You can see why it is so important to use your net worth statement as a starting point and why you should update it annually. By preparing the statement, you put yourself in a position to intelligently build for the future, based on detailed financial information about what you own and what you owe to others.

But this may not be the end of your work this day. If you have a family, you need to prepare what we call a Family Security Statement. That's a report on what your family will have to live on in the event of your untimely death.

The computations are easy, certainly as easy as preparing a net worth statement.

Begin by determining the amount of income that your family would need to live on month-to-month. You can get this by looking at the information in Lesson 8 on budgeting. Remember to elimi-

FAMILY SECURITY STATEMENT
as of (month, date, year)

*Income needed:* Sufficient for family to live on each month in the event of primary wage earner's death or disability.

_____

In case of death (70 percent of current monthly expenses)
In case of disability (100 percent of current monthly expenses)
*Income generated*
Social Security                                           _____
Income from invested life insurance proceeds             _____
Income from savings                                      _____
Income from disability insurance                         _____
Wages earned by spouse and others in family              _____
Rents and royalties                                      _____
Business income                                          _____
Income from investments (dividends and interest) _____
        TOTAL INCOME                                     _____

Compare income needed with income generated.

nate expenses that relate only to you, such as your commuting expenses, maybe a second car, extra insurance costs, and so on.

Then, in another column, begin building the income on which the family will live. Check all income sources.

Start with Social Security. The system will pay substantial amounts, especially if there are school-age children in the family. You can inquire at the Social Security Administration office about benefit levels. They are based on your covered earnings, among other factors.

Your life insurance policies will either provide a lump sum that can be invested for monthly income or pay out a regular annuity.

There are numerous life policies you should be aware of, including those from your credit union, auto policy, and clubs to which you may belong. Don't ignore them. For example, your credit union may automatically pay a couple of thousand dollars to the account of a shareholder who dies.

In addition, there are some unusual policies that surface from time to time. Although you can't count on these for financial-planning purposes, you should know they exist. For example, General Motors has a policy that pays $10,000 if you're killed in one of its cars while wearing a seat belt.

Include in the family income any salary and wages that your survivors will be earning.

Go to your tax return from the previous year and determine the amount of dividend and interest income you can expect to receive. Also calculate what may come in from rentals, royalties, and so forth.

Determine if the various business deals you are involved in will continue to produce revenue for the family and what those revenues will amount to over the years.

After you compare your family's income needs with what will come in, you will arrive at a figure. If there's a shortfall, you should plan to meet it immediately through additional financial planning—adding life insurance, changing investment strategies, and so forth. If your family will be financially well-off, your planning is done, at least for another year.


A net worth statement as well as a family security statement are not difficult to fill out, especially after you have completed your first ones. Then it's just a matter of updating the information. No amount of financial planning and money management is sufficient without these two statements.

## *Budgeting Made Easy*

Budgeting isn't tough, and it doesn't have to be time-consuming. It shouldn't take you more than an hour once each month. It's drudgery, but it does have to be done. The ideal time is when you pay your bills.

The lack of a month-to-month budget is the worst mistake that people make in their financial planning, or lack of it. Here's what a budget can do for you:

- You'll see when your income arrives and where it comes from—salary, dividends, interest, and so forth.
- You'll identify your major expenses.
- You'll note how much goes for nonessentials.
- You'll be able to see where you can reduce expenses.
- You'll identify the amount you can save.
- You'll see just how your cash flows each month.

These points are vital. Too many people live from month to month, letting their financial chips fall where they may. While that may work for a while, it's no way to get ahead financially or to plan for retirement.

We have two important points to bring up before you start:

First, if you're married, make your budget meetings a family affair. See Lesson 5 on why you and your spouse need to handle your finances together. You'll get the work done in half the time, and by using two heads on the money issues, you'll get better results.

Second, budgeting is not a form of punishment for people who cannot handle their finances. Indeed, the reason some people are so good at dealing with their money is because they have a budget, and they follow it.

Budgeting does not have to be terribly restrictive, nor does it have to be extremely precise. You don't have to keep track of every last penny. We know people who round off their budgetary figures to the nearest $100. That may be a bit much for you. But $10 or $20 may not be.

Here's how to go about developing a budget plan that works, no matter what your level of income or financial sophistication. Refer to the sample budget form at the end of this lesson, but feel free to add to it or delete from it as appropriate to your personal situation.

Start with a notebook, paper, and pencil. You can use preprinted household budget books if you like. They are available at bookstores, stationery shops, and general office supply firms. But we prefer a loose-leaf school-type notebook to which you can add paper each month. It's easy to use, and it's inexpensive.

Copy on your worksheet for the month the sample budget headings, add any others that apply, and photocopy the form for future use. Work in pencil or erasable pen. Remember, this is a working, month-to-month budget. There will be additions and deletions as your spending habits come together and as they change over the months and years.

If you have not kept a budget prior to this, we recommend that you fill out monthly reports showing your income and expenses for each of the past twelve months. This way you will have figures to compare today's numbers with, and you will also gain a clearer understanding of where your money went last year.

What if you don't have records for last year? The plain answer is that you won't be able to reconstruct your earlier financial activity. This further illustrates the need for you to keep closer track of your money. If you can even go back a couple of months, do so. It will help.

To reconstruct your past financial affairs, go to three main sources—your bank books, your credit card statements, and receipts you have saved—and transfer the figures to the appropriate months on your budget forms. These items will usually indicate when you received your income, the amounts, and the sources. They will also show the level and timing of your expenses. It's important for you to know which months you receive irregular amounts of income, like dividends, and which months you pay your annual or semiannual life and auto insurance premiums—so you can budget accordingly.

Frankly, this task—reconstructing your past finances on paper—will be time-consuming. In fact, it may take a couple of sittings to get the job done. Still, it's important. We highly recommend that you take the time to complete this essential first step in your budgeting.

Once your past year's or several months' budget is complete, you're ready to begin work on the month-to-month nitty-gritty of this year's budget. These sessions won't take long now that you've laid a sturdy foundation.

We like to have people work on three months' worth of budgets at a time. You'll spend most of your time on this month's budget, but you'll also look at last month and next month.

Start with the current month. At the top of a blank page, write down the month and year. First list, and then total, your anticipated income.

Next come your various expenses. Put your largest and most regular expenses at the top. Items such as your mortgage, car payments, and groceries come to mind. Make sure you leave space for insurance premiums, utilities, savings contributions, medical bills, credit card charges, and whatever else you spend money on each month. Now total your anticipated expenses.

Compare your income with your expenses to determine whether you have money to save or whether you will have to dip into your savings accounts to meet the bills. If you have extra income, make plans to invest it or set it aside for future bills. If you find that you'll be short of cash, see whether you can reduce some expenses.

Leave room beside your estimates so you can write down the actual amounts when they become known.

Then try to live within the budget you have set out for yourself. Leave yourself enough financial flexibility during the month so you can commute to work, buy a paper, and go to lunch if that's what you do.

The second step involves the prior month's budget. Go back through your bank accounts, checkbook registers, credit card statements, and receipts and compare your prior month's estimates with the actual expenses you incurred. Include any items you missed. Enter exact amounts beside your estimates and see how close you were to the mark. That way you will have a yardstick to measure the accuracy of your estimates. Also, if you have the records, compare your income and expenses against what you brought in and paid out during the same month one year ago.

The third stage is to set up your long-range budget for the next month. You need to remind yourself of any special income that may be due and any special expenses that will take extra money to cover. Insurance, a trip, or a big birthday or holiday present can cost you hundreds or even thousands of dollars. One way to keep up with what could otherwise surprise you is to look back in your budget book at what took place during the same month one year ago.

You'll be surprised at how enlightening this simple, three-months-at-a-glance record-keeping approach can be. It's not difficult, and it's not time-consuming. It can save you a lot of financial worry. You'll know precisely where your money is going and where it is coming from, month in and month out. You'll know, perhaps for the first time, if you are spending more than you make, or you may be surprised to find out that you have discretionary funds for investment and recreation.

The knowledge of how you have been handling your money each and every month will make you a better money manager, investor, and saver for the months ahead. You will be able to learn from past personal experience because it will be laid out in front of you. There will be no more estimating and no more guessing. Finally, you will have, at your fingertips, all the financial information you need to go about your business.

The bottom line in preparing a monthly budget is to actually use the information you learn from it. Record keeping for record keeping's sake is fruitless. But when you decide to act on the information you have gathered, you can really benefit.

## INCOME AND EXPENSES FOR
(month and year)

|  | Anticipated | Actual |
|---|---|---|
| *Income* | | |
| Wages (net) | ———— | ———— |
| Interest | ———— | ———— |
| Dividends | ———— | ———— |
| Rents | ———— | ———— |
| Other | ———— | ———— |
|   TOTAL INCOME | ———— | ———— |
| *Expenses* | | |
| Mortgage | ———— | ———— |
| Gas | ———— | ———— |
| Electric | ———— | ———— |
| Oil | ———— | ———— |
| Food | ———— | ———— |
| Trash | ———— | ———— |
| Telephone | ———— | ———— |
| Car payment | ———— | ———— |
| Gasoline | ———— | ———— |
| Charge account  No. 1 | ———— | ———— |
|   No. 2 | ———— | ———— |
|   No. 3 | ———— | ———— |
| Medical | ———— | ———— |
| Health insurance | ———— | ———— |
| Auto insurance | ———— | ———— |
| Life insurance | ———— | ———— |
| Homeowner's or rental insurance | ———— | ———— |
| Child care | ———— | ———— |
| Federal tax payment | ———— | ———— |
| State tax payment | ———— | ———— |
| Other | ———— | ———— |
|   TOTAL EXPENSES | ———— | ———— |
| Discretionary funds | ———— | ———— |
| Shortfall | ———— | ———— |

# LESSON 9

## *Preliminary Tax-Planning Session*

Tax planning doesn't take a great deal of time, but it does take some organization. January is when you should hold a preliminary session to wrap up your affairs from the year just ended and begin organizing your papers for the new one. In fact, 1987 is a particularly important year to set out new tax saving strategies for yourself. It's all because of the Tax Reform Act of 1986. You have ample opportunity to save hundreds, perhaps even thousands of tax dollars. All it takes is a little bit of advance planning on your part.

Sit down in early January to work on your tax housekeeping chores.

First, place your tax papers from the just-closed year into a shoe box or accordion file marked "Tax File (year)." Although it is not essential, you should organize your income receipts, bank statements, mortgage statements, medical bills, and other papers you have saved throughout the year that you will need when you prepare your tax return.

Watch for your tax forms in the mail as well as W-2 wage statements; 1099 income information slips; and other notices important to your tax return. Toss them into your tax folder, too.

Second, mark your new calendar with important tax dates. These include the four quarterly estimated tax payment deadlines of April 15, June 15, September 15, and the following January 15.

April 15 is also income tax day.

May 30 is when you should have received your refund.

June 15 is when your return is due if you were out of the country on April 15.

August 15 is the due date for filing your return if you file for an extension of time.

Third, mark on your calendar the four dates on which you will be planning your tax affairs throughout the year. We recommend early February, the end of June or the first of July, just after Labor Day in September, and close to Thanksgiving.

Also set aside time to prepare your return. Although you have until April 15, we recommend that you perform the annual task sometime in February.

# FEBRUARY

## *Cutting Your Tax Bill*

If you are typical, about one-third of your income goes to pay taxes over the course of a year. That's true despite the latest tax reform effort. You can save a surprising amount by following our plan.

 *To Do*

- Monthly budget
- First working tax session
  - Complete worksheets following forms on pages 53–55
  - Note future tax sessions on the calendar in June, September, November
- Fill out two tax returns, one conservative, the other aggressive
- Leave a detailed roadmap of your tax calculations: keep good records of your income, deductions, credits.
- Adjust your withholding to avoid tax refunds or prevent underpayment penalties

## *Saving on Taxes with Five Short Sessions a Year*

Tax planning doesn't have to be terribly time-consuming. You can cover everything you need to in one preliminary session and four relatively short working sessions a year, never spending more than two hours at one sitting. Follow our schedule, perform the tasks on time, and save yourself sizable chunks of tax, plus a lot of headaches at tax preparation time.

Internal Revenue Service (IRS) bureaucrats sit in their offices at their national headquarters in Washington, D.C., and plot how they will extract tax payments from you eighteen months in advance of the time you will be filing your return. In the fall of 1987, they will start planning for returns you'll be filing in 1989. If you fail to plan your tax affairs, you are at a distinct disadvantage.

Fortunately, a tax plan that should help you keep more of what you make does not have to be extraordinarily complex. You don't have to spend hour upon hour toiling over intricate tax shelters and other investments to reduce your taxes to manageable levels. We recommend that you plan your taxes during just five sessions a year, including the aforementioned short preliminary session in early January. That's all it should take.

The first tax-planning session after the preliminaries will set the tone for the other three that will come later in the year. It's at this session in early February that you need to make your basic assumptions about your income, deductions, credits, investment profits and losses, rentals, mutual funds, and so on for the next year. In other words, you need to outline your basic finances before incorporating any tax-reducing moves into your plan.

1. The starting point in developing the plan is to carefully review what transpired during the year just completed. You need to design a worksheet. Work in pencil. On one page of a legal pad, note your various sources of income from last year in one column and how you think you will do during the current year in the next column. That will provide you with a comparison throughout the year. Do the same on separate sheets for your deductions, investments, retirement accounts, and so forth. Look ahead to Lesson 11 on preparing your return for a sample worksheet you might like to use.

2. Next prepare a mock-up version of your income tax return, based on your assumptions, so you can see if you will have to pay additional tax at year's end or if you will be entitled to a refund. Use a blank copy of the previous year's IRS forms and schedules. You will have to make adjustments to reflect recent tax law changes that will affect the current year's return. (See Lesson 12 on why you don't want to qualify for a refund and Lesson 13 on the penalty for underpayments of estimated tax.) On your mock-up tax forms, make adjustments to reflect your tax situation during the current year. For example, last year you may have received a lump-sum distribution from a pension plan on which you had to pay tax. That's unlikely to happen again, so adjust this year's tax thinking to take that into account. Or you may have sold some stock-market winners. You may anticipate that you won't be selling this year.

   The key here is twofold: you must establish a starting point for your planning, and you must remain flexible. Make several copies of your mock-up tax return to use in future tax sessions.

3. Consider tax law changes that will go into effect this year. In 1987, income averaging is no longer available. Neither is the deduction for two-earner couples. Medical expenses are deductible only to the extent they exceed 7½ percent of your income. Only 65 percent of your consumer interest is deductible in 1987. The sales tax deduction is gone. Miscellaneous itemized expenses, including unreimbursed employee business expenses, are deductible only to the extent they exceed 2 percent of your income. The tax break for long-term capital gains is gone, and so may be your deduction for IRA contributions, depending on how much income you have. We can only advise you to stay as informed about changes as you can by reading the newspapers and general news magazines.

4. Some tax law changes effective in 1987 will help reduce your taxes. Tax brackets are lower and, for taxpayers who do not

itemize, the standard deduction is higher. The personal exemption rises from $1,080 in 1986 to $1,900 in 1987, $1,950 in 1988, and $2,000 in 1989; thereafter it will rise in line with inflation.

5. Make your contributions to your IRA for the current year as soon as possible, preferably in January. The maximum contribution is $2,000 for each worker. Those with spousal IRAs (that's where one spouse works and the other doesn't) can contribute $2,250 into the two accounts, with no more than $2,000 going into one account and no less than $250 going into the other. The earlier in the year you invest in these tax-saving accounts, the more rapidly they accumulate tax-deferred interest. We're assuming IRAs still make sense for you. Three out of four people can still deduct the full amount of their IRA contribution.

*Recommend early IRA contribution*

6. If you haven't made your IRA contribution for the past year, you have until April 15 to do so.

7. For self-employed individuals, you have until the time you file your return, including extensions, to make your Keogh retirement plan contributions for the past year and still deduct the contributions from your income. You can also get started on this year's contributions.

8. Scan your current investment holdings. Note those that have ✗ increased in value since you obtained them, and those that have decreased. Also note the amounts you would gain or lose if you sold each of your investments.


The second session shouldn't take you any more time than the first, and, for most people, it takes much less. It should be scheduled for late June.

1. At that time, you should revise your income and expense assumptions. The year will be close to half over. Take a look at your wage statements. You will have received half of your annual salary and half of the withholding. You've made half your mortgage payments and received half your dividends and interest. Just double the amounts. That should make plugging in new figures on your legal pad and on the mock-up tax return easy.

2. Organize the papers that you've accumulated for the first half of the year into proper categories, such as income, mortgage, charitable contributions, and so on. We like using small envelopes for this sort of thing. This saves lots of time at the start of the next year because you will have all your records organized and labeled.

3. Bring your financial calendar up to date if changes are needed. For example, say that you bought a new car. The semiannual dates for paying auto insurance will be changed.
4. Review your estimated tax liability and adjust your withholding if necessary.

The third session, in early September, will be much like the second. Again, you need to bring your legal pad and mock-up tax return up to date with current figures.

1. Organize the financial papers you received over the last three months.
2. Review your financial calendar and estimated taxes.
3. Adjust your withholding if it's called for.
4. Incorporate any securities transactions into your tax plan. If you've enjoyed gains, you may want to start looking for some offsetting losses and vice versa.

The fourth session, scheduled for the end of November, is the one that touches on year-end tax planning. Don't wait until December 15 or later to hold this. If you do, you'll find that you've run out of time to implement any reasonable year-end tax plan. The ideal time is just after Thanksgiving. Of course, you can work on this session earlier if you'd like.

1. Once again, organize your financial papers.
2. Bring your legal pad and mock-up return up to date.
3. Check on your potential tax liability for the year.
4. Consider the new tax law and its impact on your tax picture.
5. Think about shifting income into the next year so that you can delay paying income tax on it until the following April 15. This is easiest if you own and operate your own small business or if you are an investor. Small-business owners can often delay billing clients for a month or so and realize the income the next January. Investors can delay trading for a few weeks.

   Accelerating deductions from next year into this year is a relatively simple process. If you will benefit from such activities, get started early planning which bills you want to pay and where you will find the money. For example, if you owe the orthodontist $1,500, make the payment in December so it can be reported on your tax return. If you operate a small business, pay your bills before year's end.

What if you have bills that would be deductible if only you had the money to pay them? One technique that solves this problem is to borrow the funds, perhaps taking out a cash advance, and use the money to pay the tax-deductible bills. You get the deduction in the year you pay the bill, not the year you repay the loan.

6. Check on the status of any tax-saving moves you made earlier in the year, such as Treasury bills coming due or investment profits and losses, and determine if you should alter your strategies.


Tax planning isn't terribly difficult. It just takes organization. Follow our schedule and you'll never panic about your taxes again. What's more, you'll have a handle on your tax affairs throughout the year.

# LESSON 11

## *Preparing Your Tax Return*

The manner in which you prepare your income tax return goes a long way toward determining the amount of tax you pay and whether or not your return will be audited. By following our two-return approach and keeping a well-documented road map showing where each and every number on your return comes from, you will have no trouble with your taxes or the Internal Revenue Service (IRS).

When you prepare your tax return, whether alone or with a paid professional, you should anticipate that it will indeed be audited by the IRS, even though chances are excellent this won't happen. By assuming an audit, you'll take proper care in preparing the forms and schedules. And you'll develop a road map for your return, so that if and when an auditor asks where you came up with a $1,348 charitable contribution, you will be able to tell him that it was a combination of many deductions, listed on a sheet of paper and backed up by canceled checks and receipts that you've assembled.

It's important to understand the varying psychology of tax-return filing. The IRS does. If you are conservative, you don't want the IRS to challenge the return you're getting ready to prepare. Audits are time-consuming and, at times, expensive. You will probably pay a tax representative and may owe additional tax. So the prevailing attitude is, if you're getting a refund (and three out of four taxpayers do), maybe you should be cautious with the preparation of the return. And even if you owe, it might be better to pay a little extra just to keep the IRS off your back.

On the other hand, if you're aggressive about your taxes, you don't want to pay more than you have to. You need the money worse than the IRS does. So you file an aggressive return. The IRS is auditing fewer returns every year. Chances are it will never question yours.

These two positions are not nearly as far apart as you might think. That's why we recommend that you prepare not one, but two tax returns.

Fill out your first return as though an IRS auditor were looking over your shoulder every step of the way. Of course, you have to accurately report all of your income. When it comes to your deductions, take only those items you can prove beyond the shadow of a doubt. Any questionable deductions should be left off this return. Work through the forms and schedules, coming down on the IRS's side whenever there's a question. You'll reach the bottom line—the amount of your tax liability. Now put this return off to the side. You'll not be mailing it in.

Switch gears for your second return and be much more aggressive. Again, report the income that's required of you. As for your deductions and credits, claim anything and everything you think you qualify for. Remember the cash you tossed in the collection bucket for the Salvation Army at Christmas? On your first return, you claimed nothing because you don't have a receipt. On this return, claim the $10, or $20, or $50 that you contributed, even though you don't have a receipt. Again, work through your tax forms. You'll arrive at your tax liability.

Compare the tax liabilities shown on the two returns. The difference is the worst that the IRS can do to you if:

1. You file the more aggressive return, which you probably should.
2. The IRS selects your return for audit, which it probably won't, since only 1.2 percent of all returns filed are audited these days.
3. The IRS auditor identifies each questionable item on your aggressive return, which is unlikely.
4. The auditor rules against you on each of these items—again, an unlikely proposition.
5. You agree to accept the auditor's findings and not appeal the administrative decisions of the IRS.

You may be surprised at the difference between your conservative return and your aggressive one. Depending on your circumstances, it may be a terribly large amount, or it may be insignificant. Whatever the amount, if it makes you nervous, you should consider setting up a reserve in your bank account, just in case the IRS should come to call. That way, you will have the funds if you should ever have to pay. Make sure that you consider the interest you might have to pay. It should be just about the amount you are collecting on your funds on deposit.

Here's our attitude about filing a tax return. File the more aggressive return. Report all your income. Unreported income is where most of the tax problems come into play these days. It's a serious crime to purposely fail to tell the IRS what you earn. Courts put people in jail for that offense.

But when it comes to your deductions and also your interpretations of the tax law, be reasonably aggressive. Decide the close calls in your favor rather than the IRS's.

In other words, view your tax return as the first step in a business negotiation. Send in your completed forms and see if the IRS will accept your first offer. In fact, 98.8 percent of the time, it will. Wouldn't you love to have that kind of acceptance rate in your business dealings?

However, there's one more important point about preparing your return that is vital to your financial well-being. You must have a worksheet that will allow you to reconstruct your return in the event of an audit.

List

Audits take place a year or more after a return is filed. If you're like most people, your memory is not good enough to recall every financial detail that took place a couple of years ago. That's why we recommend that you leave yourself a detailed road map.

Use a legal pad. Put at the top of one page "Income for (year)." Then list your salary information from your W-2 form. Note each item of interest and where it came from, along with when it was deposited in the bank. Do the same for your dividends, investment profits, rents, royalties, and so forth. You can lean heavily on the budget sheets you developed in Lesson 8. Record all your income on this page, where it came from, when and where it was deposited, and whether or not it is taxable.

Go through each bank register to check on your deposits, making certain that you can identify those that are taxable and those that are not, which includes loans, gifts, profit on the sale of a home if you bought a more expensive one soon after. See the IRS tax booklet for a more extensive list.

The purpose of this exercise is that if you are questioned at some later date by the IRS about your dividends, for example, you can refer to your worksheet and confidently tell an auditor that you reported each and every dividend you received.

Go to another sheet and mark it "Retirement Plan Contributions." Then list the amounts you contributed during the year, the check numbers, and to which account the contributions were made.

Another page should be for "Medical Expenses." Again, indicate check numbers, what the expense is for, dates, and so forth.

Other pages could be headed "Charitable Contributions," "Interest Expenses," "Taxes Paid," "Unreimbursed Employee Business Expenses," "Miscellaneous Itemized Deductions," "Securities Transactions," and "Self-Employed Business."

Set out pages that fit your financial activities and mirror your tax return. You may ask, Do I really need a separate page for each item? No, probably not; you may want to make two or three entries on a page, especially if there is not much activity. For example, you may make only a single deposit into your retirement plan, two payments for real estate taxes, and one for state income taxes.

However you set up your road map, and whatever sheets you use, make it reflective of your return so you can go back and refer to it, perhaps years from now, and regain a feel for this year's taxes.

Once you have completed these detailed worksheets, place them with your tax file for the year. You hope that you will never have to use them. But if you are called upon to defend your return, you will be able to produce every shred of evidence to prove to an auditor that what you put down on your tax return was correct and complete.

Handling your tax return isn't tough. Fill out your conservative and your aggressive tax returns, and send in the more aggressive version. If you can, bank the difference in tax liability for a couple of years to protect yourself. If you are audited, you'll be able to defend your return with your careful records.

## SAMPLE TAX WORKSHEETS

*Income for 19___*

Include salary and wages from each job, dividends, interest, rents, royalties, investment proceeds, state tax refunds, loan proceeds, return of capital, gifts. (See the IRS booklet accompanying your tax form for a complete list.) List each item and deposit along with the following information:

| Amount | Date | Where from | When & where deposited | Taxed (Y/N) |
|--------|------|------------|------------------------|-------------|

## SAMPLE TAX WORKSHEETS (continued)

*Retirement Plan Contributions*

| Amount | Date | Check # | Type of account |
|---|---|---|---|

*Medical Expenses*

| Amount | Date | Check # | What for |
|---|---|---|---|

*Charitable Contributions*

| Amount | Date | Check # | Other receipt | To whom |
|---|---|---|---|---|

*Interest expenses*

Include mortgages and personal interest on student and car loans, credit cards, and other installment debt.

| Amount | Date | What for |
|---|---|---|

*Taxes paid*
Include state and federal withholding, personal property, real estate

| Amount | Date | What for | Deductible (Y/N) |
|---|---|---|---|

*Unreimbursed employee business expenses and other miscellaneous items*

| Amount | Check # | Type of expense | Reimbursed? (Y/N) | Deductible? (Y/N) |
|---|---|---|---|---|

*Securities transactions*

| Date of purchase | Date of sale | Tax basis | Sales price | Profit/Loss |
|---|---|---|---|---|

*Self-employed activities*

| Income: Amount | Date | From whom |
|---|---|---|

| Expenses: Amount | Check # | Notation | Deductible (Y/N) |
|---|---|---|---|

# LESSON 12

## *Why You Don't Want an Income Tax Refund*

Plan your taxes so that you and the Internal Revenue Service (IRS) break even at year's end. You don't want or need to qualify for a tax refund. That shows poor financial and tax planning on your part. It's far better for you to enjoy your hard-earned cash throughout the year than it is to grant the government an interest-free loan. Best of all, it's not difficult to put an end to the refund habit.

Currently, three out of four taxpayers overpay their income taxes throughout the year. As a result, they qualify for refunds. Some people actually believe that they aren't paying any income tax because they get a refund check from the IRS. Nothing could be further from the truth. One man argued vehemently with us that he didn't pay a dime; instead, he got a $2,500 refund. As it turns out, $17,500 was withheld from his salary during the year to cover his income tax liability. His return showed that his taxes amounted to $15,000. So the IRS issued a $2,500 refund check. He's still convinced that he doesn't pay anything to the government.

When planning your taxes for the year, you need to keep three things in mind:

1. The amount of your anticipated taxable income from all sources.
2. The amount you expect to have in tax deductions, credits, and exemptions.
3. The amount withheld from your pay, along with amounts you send in to the IRS to cover quarterly estimated taxes.

Armed with these figures and the current tax rate tables (just take a look at IRS form 1040 ES—the *ES* stands for "estimated taxes"), you can come quite close to determining your tax liability for the year.

If it looks as though you will owe the IRS, you can make arrangements with your employer to increase the amount withheld each pay period to cover your taxes. Just amend your W-4 withholding form on file at your place of employment. That way, you and the IRS will break even at year's end. Another technique is to increase your quarterly estimated tax payments to cover the shortfall. To the IRS, the definition of breaking even is when you do not owe more than $500. If you fall within this safety zone, you don't have to worry about increasing your tax payments.

On the other hand, if you calculate that you will qualify for a refund, especially a sizable one, you should take steps to correct the situation. Apply the same techniques, only in reverse. Tell your employer to reduce the amount withheld from your pay. You do this by increasing the number of withholding exemptions you claim on your W-4 withholding form. Check the instructions that go with the W-4 form so you take as many exemptions as you are legally entitled to. Or if you have been paying quarterly estimated taxes, send in less.

That's how to handle your taxes throughout the year so you break even with the IRS, but unfortunately not enough taxpayers bother to act. The proof is the number and size of refunds. Presently, the average refund to the 75 percent who overpay their taxes amounts to just about $850.

Some taxpayers actually look forward to their refunds. They view the check as an enforced savings account. They rely on the money to pay for holiday season bills, vacations, and other expenses. That's silly. You can save as easily as the government can, probably better. Just look at the way it handles its finances. If you save by yourself, at least you will earn interest on your funds.


If you need an excuse to end the refund habit, consider the following:

First, the IRS has conducted psychological studies to determine why people pay taxes and how honest they are. It has found that taxpayers who are due refunds are much less likely to be aggressive with the preparation of their returns than taxpayers who have to dig into their pockets on April 15. The IRS knows that a conservative, ultracautious taxpayer is likely to overpay even though it is unnecessary.

It's just human nature. Take this example: Last Easter, you tossed a $20 bill into the church collection plate. If you know you're due a refund as you fill out your tax return, chances are you won't claim your $20 charitable contribution simply because you don't want any trouble. You don't have a receipt, so you'll be cautious and not take the tax break you're entitled to.

But if you owe a couple of hundred dollars to the IRS, chances are you'll be more aggressive with your return. You'll take this and other deductions that you are entitled to, even though you may not have the absolute proof that you should.

Second, people complain to us that Christmas gets more difficult to afford every year. They don't have enough money. Yet these are the same people who are pleased to receive their refunds amounting to hundreds (often thousands) of dollars months after the Christmas holidays have ended. A simple change in their withholding would make life much easier.

Third, the IRS has had widely publicized problems processing refunds over the past few years. As things presently stand, it takes a minimum of six weeks from the time you file your tax return until the IRS sends out a refund check. But that's only for those who file early. Those who file later in the tax season can expect to wait at least ten weeks for their money.

If you're late filing and owe the IRS, it collects the overdue taxes plus interest back to April 15.

If you file on time (even as early as January) and are due a refund, the IRS doesn't have to OK your check until forty-five days after April 15. Even then, the check may not actually be processed until a week or two after that. All in all, the IRS can take almost two months after the filing deadline before it has to send you interest along with your refund.

Even if you do collect some interest, that's small consolation when you've needed your money. In addition, when the IRS pays interest to you, it makes sure that that interest is reported as taxable income when you file the next year. To top it off, the interest rate paid by the IRS to you is set one percentage point lower than the rate you must pay if you have a tax deficiency.

Fourth, you are depending on the U.S. Postal Service to deliver a refund check. While it generally does an excellent job handling the United States mail, there are instances where the Postal Service misses the mark. At times, the IRS sits on millions of dollars worth of undelivered refunds.

If you don't receive a refund that you've been expecting, check its status by calling the IRS.

Fifth, Congress has authorized the IRS to administer a Refund Intercept program. It works like this: You file your return, and it calls for a refund. But before the check is processed, IRS's computers see if you have any delinquent student loans; unpaid court-ordered child care; or past-due Veterans Administration, Small Business Administration, or other federal loans. The computers also check to see if you owe any outstanding state or local taxes. If you do, they are paid first out of your tax refund. You get anything left over. Only after checking all of these sources will the IRS process your refund.

 No, you don't want a tax refund. You want your money as you earn  it throughout the year. It's much better to have your cash in hand than it is to depend on the IRS to return to you what is already yours.

# LESSON 13

## *Estimated Taxes and Proper Withholding*

While you don't want to pay more tax during the year than you must, you certainly don't want to underpay the Internal Revenue Service (IRS) to the extent that you are slapped with a penalty for underpayment of estimated tax. You can hit the mark with your tax payments. All it takes is an understanding of the rules.

Growing numbers of savvy taxpayers are reducing their withholding and quarterly estimated tax payments in an effort to eliminate their refunds. Although they certainly have the right idea—letting their excess tax money work for them rather than for the IRS—some are cutting the corner just a bit too sharply. When that happens, an impersonal IRS computer sends out a notice, charging a penalty that has run from a low of 6 percent to a high of 20 percent over the years. Because of tax reform, the rate is adjusted quarterly and is based on market rates of U.S. Treasury securities.

Fortunately, the penalty for underpayment of estimated tax is easy to avoid. Here's how:

- Anticipate this year's estimated tax liability by calculating your income and deductions and then applying the tax rates in effect for the year to your taxable income.
- Add the amounts of withheld income taxes and estimated taxes you will have paid during the year. Use the amount withheld shown on your pay stub and multiply that by the number of pay periods. Add to that total the amount you pay in quarterly payments and compare your figure with what you calculate your taxes will be.

If the shortfall is under $500, you have no problem. As noted in Lesson 12, the IRS assesses no penalties if you owe less than $500.

If you owe more than that, you have two options. You can either increase your payroll withholding and/or estimated tax payments, or you can qualify under an exception to the penalty, which is detailed below.

As a reminder, you can increase the amounts withheld from your salary check at any time by visiting your personnel office and asking for a new W-4 withholding form. There are explicit instructions attached to the form explaining precisely how many exemptions you should claim, based on your income, anticipated tax deductions, and credits. If you want more income tax withheld so as to avoid the underpayment penalty, claim fewer exemptions than you do currently. Your employer will withhold more tax; your paycheck will shrink. It's that simple. You can file an amended W-4 form as many times during the year as necessary.

To compute the exact amount that you need to pay in estimated taxes to avoid any penalty, take 90 percent of your anticipated tax liability for the year (it used to be 80 percent before tax reform changed it). Then subtract the amounts that will be withheld from salary checks. The remainder is what you must cover in estimated taxes. Divide this amount by four and make equal payments by the required dates of April 15, June 15, September 15, and the following January 15. As long as 90 percent of your annual tax liability is covered through withholding and quarterly estimated tax payments, you won't be hit with an underpayment penalty.

Or you can forget about the entire underpayment penalty problem by wiggling through a loophole in the tax law untouched by the 1986 Tax Reform Act: namely, pay in withholding and estimated taxes an amount equal to or greater than last year's tax liability.

Look up your tax liability on last year's tax return. Then make sure that the sum of this year's withholding and estimated tax payments equals or exceeds that amount. Do that, and the IRS can't charge you with underpaying your estimated taxes.

For example: Say your tax liability was $8,000 last year. This year has been an extremely good one, and you expect that your taxes will come to $15,000 despite reductions in the tax rates. One of the reasons you've enjoyed this success is that you made a killing in the stock market, and that income is not subject to income tax withholding. Withholding from your pay will come to $10,000, leaving you $5,000 short at tax time next April.

You need not pay the IRS one more dime during the year, because this year's withholding exceeds last year's taxes. You will, of course, have to come up with the other $5,000 at tax time.

Let's change the example just a bit. Again, last year you paid

$8,000 in tax, and this year you expect to owe $15,000. But now, your withholding comes to only $6,000. In this instance, you need to pay at least $2,000 in estimated taxes during the year. That's $500 each quarter. This way, your withholding and estimated taxes ($6,000 and $2,000) will total last year's tax bill, and you will have sidestepped the underpayment penalty.

True, on April 15, you'll have to come up with $7,000 (that's a $15,000 tax liability minus $6,000 in payroll withholding and $2,000 in estimated tax). But that's better than paying the tax early. Bank that $7,000 at 6 percent annual interest. It's better that you should have it than the IRS.

What happens if your income (and taxes) this year will be less than last year? In this case, you won't be able to use the loophole.

There are any number of additional reasons you may need to increase your income tax or estimated tax payments during the year. You may have received a large sum of unanticipated taxable money that's not subject to withholding, such as the capital gain from the sale of an investment. Rental and royalty income also fall into this category.

Self-employed individuals have no withholding from salary checks; they must make quarterly estimated payments to cover their taxes for the year based on their net self-employment income. Also, income from operating partnerships is not subject to withholding.

Congress toughened the rules on underpaying estimated taxes when it overhauled taxes in 1986. Now you must pay at least 90 percent of your current taxes, or 100 percent of last year's, to escape the penalty and the penalty rate itself is adjusted quarterly instead of semi-annually, so watch this tax pitfall carefully.

# *Our Easiest and Most Important Tax Tip—Keep Good Records*

The easiest and most important tax tip we can give you is to keep good records. As long as you maintain a well-organized and complete record-keeping system to keep track of your financial papers, you will have no difficulty with the Internal Revenue Service (IRS). In fact, instead of being a burdensome chore, you'll find, most likely, that you will save money by cutting your taxes.

It's a fact. The IRS collects millions (maybe even billions) of dollars every year that it is not legally entitled to. The reason is simple. Taxpayers are forced to pay tax deficiencies plus interest, and sometimes even fines and penalties, because when audited they cannot back up what they report on their income tax returns with records, receipts, and other types of proof.

It's not a question of cheating but rather one of record keeping. For example, say you anonymously donate $100 in cash to your alma mater. You have no proof that you made the gift, and the school has no record of its coming from you. What happens if you report the $100 gift when you file your return? Chances are, nothing. After all, only 1.2 percent of all returns filed are seriously questioned by the IRS. But if you are audited, the IRS agent will most likely ask you to provide proof of your charitable contributions. When you aren't able to back up your claim, you will have to pay a tax deficiency and interest, and possibly a penalty, too.

There are important pluses to becoming a complete record keeper:

First, chances are you will pay less tax because of good records. Prior to becoming a complete record keeper, you probably would have forgone valuable tax benefits simply because you couldn't come up with the receipts to prove them. Armed with solid records, you will most likely be able to claim larger deductions than in years past. For example, if you operate your own firm, you can easily lose track of the numerous out-of-pocket expenses you incur every day.

Second, you will no longer have an uneasy feeling about your tax return, especially those areas that have been shot down (either by the IRS or by your tax preparer) in years past because of inadequate records. You will know that you can prove every last dollar you claim when you file.

On the flip side, there are two reasons people use to justify (at least in their own minds) lax record keeping. First is the audit lottery. People know that their overall audit risk is quite low. And since there's every possibility that they won't be questioned about their taxes, they get sloppy and lazy about keeping their tax records in good order.

That's the financial version of Russian roulette. People rationalize that with the audit odds so low, why go to all the trouble of keeping good records? Even those taxpayers reporting income of well over $50,000 a year are not audited to any great extent. Their audit risk is less than one in ten.

You should anticipate that you will be audited—every year. Then, if your return is selected, you can confidently face the IRS and walk away from the confrontation unscathed.

Second, the IRS has a reputation for compromise, so people rationalize that even if they are hit by an audit, they won't be hit too hard. It's true, the IRS does compromise, even though it puts on a stern face to the taxpaying public. However, the tax law has always required taxpayers to verify their business-related expenses for travel and entertainment and to have proof of their charitable contribution deductions, medical expenses, tax and interest payments, and the like. For example, if you drive your car on business, the IRS will demand that you prove either your mileage or your business driving expenses. If you have insufficient proof, you stand to be assessed a tax deficiency.

But it's rarely all or nothing. While an auditor has the authority to deny all tax breaks that you cannot absolutely prove, that rarely happens. For example, say you deduct $8,000 in travel and entertainment expenses on your tax return but can only nail down $5,000 with absolute proof. If audited, chances are the IRS examiner would let you take $1,000 to $1,500 of the additional $3,000 you claimed. Of course, that's assuming the rest of the audit went well for you, that you could prove most of the other tax breaks you claimed when you filed. In other words, there's a lot of quiet negotiating that goes on during an audit. It's easier that way. "I'll let you have $1,000 in deductions if you agree to give up the other $2,000 that you claimed but can't absolutely prove." If auditors didn't negotiate, tax-return examinations would drag on forever. The IRS would have an even bigger backlog than it currently carries.

In this example, the taxpayer might get a $1,000 deduction even without solid proof. However, if proper records had been maintained, the tax deduction would have been for the full amount.


Become a complete record keeper for tax purposes. It's not difficult or even terribly time-consuming. You can use a legal pad, a file drawer, and a set of envelopes appropriately marked. It's that simple. You will want to keep copies of your last few tax returns handy, along with the worksheet from last year's return. That way you will have something to guide you as you organize your tax plans and papers. Refer to Lesson 10 on holding five quick and easy tax-planning sessions a year.

The system you use is entirely up to you. Make it one that is easy to handle. You needn't put the information on a computer, although if that makes it easier for you to calculate, go ahead. However, remember that you will need to keep track of all the paper documents that support your deductions.

In Lesson 8, we talked about the type of financial record-keeping system you need to handle your month-to-month budget. That can serve as a starting point for your tax record-keeping system. Although the two systems are similar, they are not exactly alike. For example, in your monthly budget, you have line items for your utility bills. But they are not tax items. In your monthly budget, you have line items for each of your charge accounts. In your tax worksheets and folders, you should break out only those specific credit card charges that are directly related to tax matters, such as charged medical visits and state tax payments.

The lists we recommend are easy to maintain. A loose-leaf notebook or legal pad is all you need. As covered in previous lessons, keep separate lists for your income, deductions, and credits. Sort your various sources of income so you are certain you know where all your money (taxable and nontaxable alike) is coming from during the year—wages, dividends, interest, investment profits, tax-free gifts, municipal bond interest, transfers between your various accounts, and so on. Record in your checkbook registers the sources of your deposits. You wouldn't want to mistakenly pay tax on a transfer, so mark it according to which account the money is coming from and which it is going to. Along the same lines, note nontaxable deposits such as the return of capital from an investment and loan proceeds that you deposit in your account.

Maintain the same kind of detailed sheets and envelopes for your mortgage interest, Individual Retirement Account contributions (whether or not your contribution is deductible), unreimbursed employee business expenses, and the like.

You should also keep permanent tax files covering your investments, gifts you have made and received, and your personal residence.

It's not hard to keep complete tax records. The nice thing about them is that once you get into the swing of writing down your income and deductions, you'll find that you will pay the IRS no more than it is entitled to. The IRS will continue to collect extra money from the bad record keepers, but not from you.

Good record keeping

A. Files or folders for separate items

1. Year d; tem

# MARCH

## *More Tax Tips*

Taxes figure into every financial decision of the smart money manager, from investing to charitable giving.

 *To Do*

- Monthly budget
- If you need more time, ask the IRS for an automatic extension of time to file (see page 69)
- Throw out any unneeded old tax records

# *Paying Your Taxes Late, Legally*

Sit back and feel sorry for those unfortunate souls fighting their way to the post office on April 15 in order to meet the midnight filing deadline for individual income tax returns. You needn't be one of them.

April 15 has traditionally been known as income tax day. That's when you are to file your annual Form 1040 and settle up with the Internal Revenue Service (IRS). The fact is, more than one-half of all taxpayers send in their returns well before the filing deadline. And, as we've mentioned previously, three out of four taxpayers qualify for refunds. It's no wonder that people file well before April 15. The earlier you file, the faster you can expect to receive your money.

But for the millions of savvy people who plan their tax affairs so that they do not qualify for refunds but rather break even with the IRS at year's end, there is no incentive to file early. (To repeat, the IRS definition of breaking even is when the taxpayer owes no more than $500 in additional tax for the year.)

If you owe additional tax, no matter how small an amount, you may, for strategic reasons, want to postpone the day of reckoning as long as you legitimately can. Here are a number of techniques and strategies used for years by taxpayers who want or need to put off the IRS.

First, file for an automatic extension of time by sending in a completed IRS Form 4868 no later than April 15. This will garner you an automatic four additional months to complete your tax return for the year. The extension form only provides you with additional time to complete your return. It is not intended to grant you extra time to pay your taxes. But in fact it does, at least for a small portion of what you owe.

Form 4868 calls for you to estimate the amount of your tax liability for the year based on your income, deductions, and credits. Then, after adding the amounts that have been withheld from your salary checks to cover your federal income taxes and any estimated tax payments you may have made during the year, you subtract that total from your tax liability. If you find that it's likely you'll owe more tax, you must pay it when you file Form 4868 by April 15. If the calculations show that it's likely you'll get a refund, just send in Form 4868 without a check.

But how can people determine their tax liability for the year when their tax returns have yet to be completed? The IRS says that you should just do the best you can. Make your best "guesstimate." As long as what you have paid totals at least 90 percent of what your tax liability finally turns out to be after you complete your return some months later, you'll be OK. No fines, no penalties. Of course, you'll have to pay the tax shortfall. But at least you get a four-month extension of time to pay that amount.

For example, say your preliminary figures show that your taxes for the year will amount to $8,000, and at least that amount was withheld from your salary checks during the year. You mail in your Form 4868 by April 15; you don't need to include a check.

It later turns out that your tax for the year should have been $8,800. Just send in your check for the extra $800 by mid-August. You fall within the 10 percent safe harbor. You have delayed paying at least some tax using this technique. You'll have to pay interest but no penalty. The IRS will send you a bill for the interest.

If you miss the 10 percent safe harbor, you can be penalized, so it's a good idea to work carefully on your estimate to make sure you don't fall short of the mark.

The second delaying tactic is to let the IRS calculate your taxes for you. Short-form filers can qualify for this tactic quite easily. Long-form filers have a tougher time because they can't itemize their deductions on Schedule A, plus there are other restrictions.

Note on your tax forms the amount of your income (don't forget to attach your W-2 wage forms), any interest income you have, the amounts withheld for income tax payments, that sort of thing. Then, continuing your calculations as called for on the form you are getting ready to send in, come up with a taxable-income figure. At that point, stop. Sign your incomplete return and mail it. The IRS will perform the final calculations for you. The instructions on how to get the IRS to calculate your tax liability for you are spelled out in detail in the instruction booklet sent to you by the IRS at the beginning of each tax season.

Submit your form on April 15, and the IRS will figure your taxes and send you a bill. That will take about a month. You will have at least two weeks to send in your check for what you owe. This works pretty well if you want to hold on to your money for a couple of extra months.

Third, if it's convenient, and you can afford the luxury of a day off from work, you can always arrange to be out of the country on April 15. The law is quite explicit. Any American taxpayer who is out of the country on April 15 is automatically granted a two-month extension of time to file and pay. In Detroit, it has become "Take Your Spouse to Lunch in Windsor, Ontario, Day" after this little ploy was announced some years ago on Detroit radio. People in San Diego trek across the border into Mexico. So do Texans. New Yorkers living in Buffalo cross the Peace Bridge into Canada. But be careful. Don't go to Puerto Rico or the U.S. Virgin Islands. Even though these are terrific places to visit, they are considered part of the United States.

Also, if you are married and filing jointly, only one of you needs to be in a foreign land on April 15, although it would be nice to bask together at a luxury resort knowing that you have an extra two months to settle with the IRS. If you are married and filing separately, then only you have to be away; it doesn't matter where your spouse is, since you are not filing together.

How can a person prove he or she was out of the country on April 15? Any reasonable receipt will do. It may be a restaurant charge slip showing the date. Or even a bill of sale from a shop. There is no requirement that you notify the IRS about your trip prior to April 15, and there is no official tax form to fill out. Just attach a note to your return when you file by June 15 stating that you were out of the country on income tax day. The IRS may not like it, but you won't be in any trouble. You'll just have to pay any additional tax you might owe, along with interest on the tax debt.

The fourth postponement approach is a double-barreled one: you can combine the two-month grace period for those out of the country with the four-month extension of time, but the total still only comes to four months. By mid-June, file Form 4868 asking for more time. Remember, it's automatic. You don't have to get the IRS to agree to the extension. You can stretch out the filing deadline until mid-August.

We should note that if you owe more tax, you must pay interest on the deficiency at a rate pretty close to the market rate paid on short-term U.S. Treasury securities. You might well ask, then, what's the advantage in putting off your tax payments, especially because there is every chance that you will forget important financial events that transpired during the year in question? A bad memory often means that you forget to claim valuable tax breaks.

While not everyone benefits from tax delay, there are significant advantages to certain people.

1. The procrastinator who finds himself right up against the April 15 filing deadline needs the additional time to bail himself out of a mess.
2. The investor who carefully watched the calendar was able to use this trick. Unfortunately, it was ended by the Tax Reform Act of 1986. Profits on sales of securities held for more than six months qualified for favorable long-term capital gain treatment. When an investor sold securities at a profit between Christmas and New Year's, she could elect when to declare the profit and pay the tax on the transaction. You had two options: you could declare your gain in the year of the sale or in the next year. The longer you delayed making that choice, the more likely you would be to know the level of your income for the current year. Say your 1986 income amounted to $40,000. In addition, you sold some stock for cash on December 28, 1986, for a $10,000 long-term capital gain. You put off filing your 1986 return and find that 1987 is shaping up as a very good year, with income anticipated at $60,000. You will obviously want to declare your year-end stock profit in 1986 because your 1986 income will be taxed in a lower bracket than in 1987.
3. The taxpayer who owes more tax frequently has better use for his money than sending it in prematurely to the IRS.

Those who owe fall into two groups: those who have the cash available to send in and those who do not.

If you owe but cannot pay, you can buy additional time to raise funds to pay your tax debt. The price is the interest you will have to pay on your tax debt. By utilizing legal delaying tactics, you avoid costly late-filing and late-payment penalties, even if you do wind up paying some interest on the amount you owe. That interest is no longer fully deductible.

If you owe and can pay, why not send in your return and check, and be done with the chore of filing your taxes? Say you can invest your funds at a greater rate of return than that being charged by the IRS. We are not advocating that you put your tax money into risky investments. Far from it. However, if the IRS is charging 9 percent, and you can earn 11 percent, you would be foolish to cash in an investment early.

Take this example: You own a certificate of deposit (CD) or Treasury security that matures August 1. You intend to use the money to pay your taxes. If you cash the CD early, you will most likely be subject to a bank penalty for early withdrawal. If you sell the Treasury security on the open market, you may suffer a loss as well as having to pay unnecessary commissions. It's wiser to hold on to your investment until maturity and pay your taxes plus interest at that time.

You have every opportunity to pay your taxes and file your return well after the traditional April 15 filing deadline. Just don't run afoul of IRS fines and penalties. They are easy enough to sidestep. And remember, the later you file, the better opportunity you have to devise a detailed tax-saving plan throughout this year and next.

# LESSON 16

## *Tax-Smart Charitable Giving*

Go ahead and give to worthwhile charities. Just make sure you do so the taxwise way.

The federal government is continuing to cut back on many worthwhile social and charitable programs. It's not because federal bureaucrats are miserly or mean-hearted but rather that the price tag is simply too high in this time of enormous budget deficits. Without government funding and support, the needy are looking to private charitable and similar organizations for help. The call is out for you to give, and give generously.

Once you decide which organizations you wish to support, or continue to support, and in what amounts, it is then time to learn the tax rules—in detail. Not surprisingly, the Internal Revenue Service (IRS) has passed regulations covering the ins and outs of charitable giving, frequently adding new wrinkles to this tax break.

To qualify for a tax deduction, your contributions can be made only to certain groups. They include charitable, educational, governmental, and similar organizations. At first glance, you might think this list covers just about everyone and everything you might contribute to, but it doesn't. For example, contributions to a social club are not deductible even though the club is tax-exempt. And you can't write off what you give to your homeowners' association. If you are not positive your contribution will qualify for tax-deduction purposes, ask a financial officer of the organization. If the answer you receive is a bit vague, or you're still not sure, call the IRS. It keeps a master list of qualifying groups.

Some people object to the idea of making a generous gift on the one hand but then claiming a tax break for it on the other. The fact is, because of the income tax benefits, you can often afford to be doubly generous. If you made a charitable donation in 1986 when income tax rates were significantly higher than they are today, then you would have enjoyed a larger tax benefit. Now that tax rates are lower, the tax breaks for giving are reduced.

Say you have decided to give $1,000 to a worthwhile organization you know is tax-qualified. If you made the gift in 1986 and were in a 50 percent tax bracket, you would have enjoyed a $500 tax benefit. You, in effect, gave $500 and the IRS chipped in the other $500. If you truly wanted to make a full $1,000 gift, you could have given $2,000. That way, the charity would have received $2,000–$1,000 directly out of your pocket and another $1,000 courtesy of the IRS.

But now tax brackets are down. Say you are in the 35 percent tax bracket in 1987. In that case, a $1,000 tax-deductible donation (assuming you itemize) results in a $350 tax savings. The net cost of your gift, after taxes, is $650.

And if you are in the 28 percent tax bracket, that $1,000 gift costs you $720 and the IRS pays $280.

Despite changes to the tax rates, you still have a silent partner in the Internal Revenue Service.

The latest changes in the tax laws will have an important impact on charitable giving. The increase in the standard deduction will mean that fewer people than ever will file Schedule A, listing their itemized deductions such as charity, medical, mortgage interest, and taxes. If you don't itemize, you can't deduct your charitable donations. 1986 was the last year that nonitemizers were allowed any tax benefit for their generosity.

Essentially, there are four categories for charitable contributions:

1. Cash.
2. Property worth less than $500. Property includes land, jewels, cars, clothes, books, art objects, and so on.
3. Property valued between $500 and $5,000.
4. Property worth more than $5,000.

Each requires a significantly different tax treatment.

*For cash,* you must keep a written receipt, such as a canceled check or letter acknowledging the gift, to verify your contribution. It must show the name of the organization, the date of the gift, and, of course, the amount. If you don't have a written receipt, you are permitted to reconstruct one after the gift has been made, but it's not the safest thing to do. That's because the burden is on you, if an auditor should require it, to prove you made the gift in the amount you claim. Auditors are suspicious by nature. The best bet when contributing cash is to pay by check. If you use cash, make sure that you get a receipt signed by a member of the group at the time of the donation. Otherwise, you may, if audited, be assessed a tax deficiency for lack of verification.

*For property worth less than $500,* you should get a signed receipt from the charity that lists the name of the organization, the date of the gift, and a description of the property. The IRS also wants to see a dollar value placed on the goods by the charity. But that rarely happens. Most of the charities use volunteers. Even paid employees are reluctant to put their name on the dotted line and attest to the value of your donated items. Fortunately, there is an alternative. You should mark down what you feel is the fair market value. Color snapshots often help your case if you are audited.

*For property worth between $500 and $5,000,* you need all the information listed in the item above as well as a written record of how and when you acquired the property and your cost or other tax basis in it. A copy of the purchase receipt would suffice.

You are now also required to attach special tax Form 8283 ("Noncash Charitable Contribution Appraisal Summary") to your Form 1040, showing the details of your charitable contributions involving property valued in this dollar range.

*For property worth more than $5,000,* you will need to hire a reputable appraiser prior to making the gift. He or she will need to sign the appraisal information on Form 8283, which you will have to send to the IRS when you file.

The IRS has long perceived that a great deal of cheating has been attempted by taxpayers who claim to make charitable contributions of valuable property when in fact the contributions are worth far less than what is stated. There have been cases where taxpayers have claimed hundreds of thousands of dollars for contributions of real estate, gems, paintings, and other works of art, while the IRS contends that the true value is only a tenth of what was listed.

The newest rules require that within 60 days prior to making a gift of valued property (defined as worth more than $5,000), you must hire a reputable appraiser who was unassociated both with the original purchase of the property and with this disposition of it. The cost of the appraisal is tax-deductible as a miscellaneous itemized deduction on Schedule A. The appraiser must sign IRS Form 8283, which you will file. Without this form properly filled out, charitable contributions of property valued at more than $5,000 are forfeited.

The appraisal will cover a description of the property, its condition, the date of the contribution, the name and other identifying information of the appraiser or her firm, the appraiser's qualifications, the date the property was valued, a statement that the appraiser knows the work is being done for income tax purposes, and the method of valuation used.

There's another new wrinkle you need to know about concerning donations greater than $500. Frequently, charities raise money by holding auctions. They ask for donations of property, which they then sell to the highest bidder. You might give some valued property to the charity, even having it appraised prior to making the gift. Then the charity sells it at auction. Or you might contribute to a museum and the museum then sells the gift to raise money for other exhibits.

In either case, you could face a serious tax problem. The new IRS rules require that when a charity sells a property within two years of the time it was acquired, it must notify the IRS of: the name, address, and taxpayer identification number of both the donor and the donee; a description of the property; the date of the contribution; and the amount the charity received when it disposed of the property.

A problem could develop if your appraiser has valued the painting, for example, at $10,000, which you have claimed on your taxes, and the auction price is a mere $2,000.

There is one exception. If you as a donor tell the charity that the property is worth $500 or less, the charity is let off the hook. It is not required to notify the IRS about the later disposition of the property.

The IRS is tightening up on the record-keeping rules for charitable deductions. It's sure to be a hot audit trigger for years to come. Yet if you are armed with the records and receipts necessary to verify your generosity, you won't have any trouble with the IRS. In fact, you can enlist the tax agency in your favorite causes by enjoying your tax deductions for charitable donations.

*what to keep*

# Dumping Musty Old Tax Records

It's probably past time to clean out the bulk of your old tax files. For the most part, you needn't keep them for more than three years after you file your return. But be aware there are some records you need to keep forever.

Every year, you pore through your financial records in order to prepare your income tax return. You use information from your checkbook registers, investment accounts, mutual fund reports, credit card statements, mortgage records, banks, and other sources. You may hold on to canceled checks, utility bills, and all those other miscellaneous scraps of paper that come in the mail throughout the year.

Once the tax returns are filed, many people toss all these papers, along with a copy of their federal and state tax returns, into a shoe box or other depository and put it on an out-of-the-way shelf in the basement or a closet, never again to see the light of day.

At least that's the hope. After all, why would anyone voluntarily go looking for old tax records? One of the very few reasons we can think of is because an Internal Revenue Service (IRS) tax examiner has come to call.

For most people, old records will stay on the shelf where they belong, out of sight and out of mind. That's fine. But if you begin keeping tax papers when you start filing returns, you can accumulate a lot of shoe boxes over the years. An individual might start filing at age twenty-two. By the time he or she reaches sixty-five, there's an awful lot of space being taken up by old tax records.

So take some time to clear out the closet. Here's what you need to know about how long you must keep your income tax records.

The primary rule is that the IRS has up to three years from the time a return is filed or its due date, whichever is later, to audit that return. You live by the same rule; you have as long as three years to file an amended return if you should find that you overlooked a tax break or two. For example, let's assume you filed your

1985 income tax return on or before its due date of April 15, 1986. The IRS has until April 15, 1989, to take a crack at it. So write on the top of that tax shoe box, "Discard after April 15, 1989."

While the IRS uses this general three-year statute of limitation for auditing returns, it can look over returns that go back six years if you failed to report more than 25 percent of your income. That's why it is so important for you to be able to prove that you reported all your income. If you never filed a return in the first place, the IRS is not restricted in the time it can question you about your financial activity.

Say that you are reading this sometime in early 1987. You should think about tax returns filed for 1982 and earlier. That 1982 return was filed by April 15, 1983. Three years later is April 15, 1986, and that's past. Accordingly, every shoe box for tax records from 1982 and earlier is a candidate for the trash pile.

The box full of tax records for 1983 can be discarded once April 15, 1987, comes and goes. The box for 1984 can go after April 15, 1988.

However, don't toss away all of those old, musty papers without opening the boxes. There is a handful you should extract from each year's tax records and place in a tax drawer marked "Permanent Tax Records."

Search through each shoe box for the following items:

1. Checkbook registers. They don't take up much room and can be instrumental in reconstructing financial dealings if that's ever required.
2. A copy of the tax returns filed for the year. That includes your federal return, and state and local returns if required.
3. Along with the returns, keep the W-2 wage forms, 1099 income information slips, and other reports of income you received during the year.
4. Data on investment activities. This should be placed in its own permanent folder marked "Investments." The information you keep on old investments can have a bearing on the current basis of your securities, real estate, and the like. It's to your advantage to have precise data on investments so you can accurately calculate any gain or loss on the eventual sale.
5. Data on gifts. You may have received a number of valuable gifts over the years—things like securities, real estate, and other property. Again, you need to be able to provide evidence of your

tax basis in the property when you report the sale, possibly years from now. Mark a folder "Gifts."

6. Data on your personal residence. Your "House" file should contain the closing papers you received at settlement and receipts for all capital improvements you have made. If you have purchased and sold more than one house over the years, you should have tax records on all of them in this file.

7. A select few canceled checks, particularly those used to pay taxes. This is solid evidence you paid federal, state, and local taxes.

Everything else can be pitched into the trash, and that usually amounts to a sizable pile of paper. Toss out your utility payments, credit card charges, receipts and records for cash payments, bank statements, most canceled checks, and whatever else you have stuffed into your tax box.

For those few boxes of tax records that are still sitting on the shelf, you might want to go through each one and separate the records you intend to keep permanently from those you will be throwing away when the three years are up. Place a rubber band around the papers you will save, so when the time comes, you can get rid of yet another unneeded box of tax records.

# APRIL

## *Smart Investing*

Smart investing is not difficult and does not require a lot of time. If you use the reliable and straightforward investments we recommend, you'll build wealth without worry. Work an investment program into your budget and watch your net worth grow.

 *To Do*

- Monthly budget
- If you have not filed for an extension, your tax return, with payment, must be postmarked by April 15
- Call for brochures on the mutual funds we recommend (see pages 97–98)
- Buy Schabacker's Mutual Fund Quarterly Performance Review (see page 96)
- Plan your business trips over the summer so you can take advantage of tax deductible vacations (see page 172)

# The Basics of Investing

Don't let the jargon confuse you. Here are the investments you need to know about.

Different investments are tailored for different goals. Here's a breakdown:

GOAL: GROWTH

*Growth* and *capital gain* are fancy words for profit. Money you invest for growth has to be money you don't need now and won't need for some time. Growth investments are designed to grow in value over the long haul, even though they may decline in value in any given month or year.

Most growth investments pay little or no yield (*yield* means interest or dividends). So when you invest for growth, you are saying good-bye to your money now, in the expectation that it will grow substantially in value—that you'll reap greater profits over the long haul than if you simply put your money in a savings account or a certificate of deposit.

You get no guarantees. To varying degrees, growth investments are risky. We recommend two kinds of growth investments:

*Equity mutual funds. Equity* is a synonym for stock. An equity mutual fund is a mutual fund that owns shares of stock in a number of companies. Over the long haul, stocks have consistently produced impressive growth. A mutual fund lessens the risk, through diversification (a bunch of stocks instead of just one) and professional management. Some of the best mutual funds invest in stocks based entirely on their prospects for growth. Never buy shares in a mutual fund from a broker. Brokers charge you a hefty commission, or "load"; besides, many of the best mutual funds are sold only by mail order. (See Lesson 21.)

*Real estate.* Like stocks, real estate has historically produced fine growth. First and foremost, we recommend that you own your own home (see Lesson 35). Two other kinds of real estate investments are worth considering. One is a house or condo or office building that you buy and rent out—an investment that provides attractive tax benefits in addition to potential growth (see Lesson 34). The other is a real estate investment trust, or REIT, which is like a mutual fund, except that it owns rental properties rather than stocks (see Lesson 33). The new tax law enhances the appeal of REITs.

GOAL: INCOME

When you deposit money in a bank or savings institution, you are paid interest. You have made an income-producing investment. If you want instant access to your money, you'll get paid less interest than if you commit your money for a year or two years or five years: the longer the period, the higher the interest rate.

That's entirely fair, because inflation gradually lessens the value of your money. For example, let's say you commit $1,000 for five years, at 8 percent interest, and inflation averages 4 percent. You're paid $80 a year—8 percent of $1,000—and at the end of five years you get your $1,000 back. But your $1,000 won't buy as many goods as it would have five years before, because inflation has raised prices. Your 8 percent investment has yielded you a "real return" of 4 percent—8 percent interest minus 4 percent inflation.

In a bank or savings institution, those fixed-term savings accounts are called certificates of deposit—CDs. Accounts that give you instant access to your money are called money market accounts. In a federally insured bank, savings institution, or credit union, your accounts and CDs are insured up to $100,000. If the bank goes bust, Uncle Sam pays you.

If you want a little more interest, you can buy into a bond mutual fund rather than buying a CD. Bonds are a little riskier than CDs, so they pay a little more interest. Municipal bonds—"munis"—usually pay a little less interest than other bonds, but muni interest is exempt from federal income tax.

Everyone should keep some cash in an insured money market account or a money market mutual fund. Beyond that, we recommend three kinds of income investments:

*Insured certificates of deposit.* Buy only from banks or savings institutions that pay the very highest interest rates. (See Lesson 27.)

*Short-term bond mutual funds.* The long-term funds pay higher yields but carry more risk. Buy only "no-load" funds (*no-load* means no sales commission). Pick from the funds listed in Lesson 27. Unless your tax bracket is very low, choose a muni fund.

*Single-premium whole life insurance.* No, we're not scrambling lessons. Single-premium whole life is an investment that yields tax-exempt interest. It's a life insurance policy, too, but that's secondary. It sounds crazy, but it works, and it was not touched by the new tax law. (See Lesson 28.)

## GOAL: GROWTH AND INCOME

Some stocks pay good dividends and also offer prospects for growth. We recommend two kinds of growth–plus–income investments:

*Mutual funds.* In Lesson 21, see the list of "Funds Seeking Income with Moderate Growth."

*REITs.* That's the acronym for real estate investment trusts. (See Lesson 33.)

## GOAL: NEST EGG FOR RETIREMENT

Individual Retirement Accounts (IRAs) and other retirement accounts are generously sheltered from federal income tax, and were not as severely curtailed by the new tax law as many people were led to believe. These tax provisions alter the usual equations. (See Lessons 50 and 51.)

## GOAL: COLLEGE MONEY

Again, tax laws play a large part in building a college nest egg. Two laws enacted in late 1986 present new problems—and new opportunities—in paying for college. (See Lesson 38.)

You can use the same straightforward, do-it-yourself investments to meet other financial goals. If you understand your goals, you can put together the financial tools to attain them, using the lessons in this book. No "expert" will understand your goals as well as you do or care as much about your progress toward achieving them.

## Never, Never Try to Predict
## the Stock Market

No one can predict the course of the stock market, so don't try.

Invest regularly in proven stock mutual funds and ride out the

market cycles.

The proposition is tempting: if you could predict when the market would rise and when it would fall, you could switch in and out of stocks and make barrels of money. *Forbes*, one of the best financial magazines, calculated that anyone with that kind of wisdom could have multiplied his or her money 22-fold during the decade that ended in December 1983.

But nobody did. Not that people didn't try. "Market timing," as the practice is called, is the most virulent infection on Wall Street—"the impossible dream," *Forbes* termed it. A whole industry has built up around market timing. On the popular television program "Wall Street Week," Louis Rukeyser mischievously refers to market-timing technicians as the "elves." So many market-timing newsletters are published, each with its own impressively incomprehensible equations, that another newsletter keeps track of the market-timing newsletters. Even the daily stock-market stories in local newspapers and *The Wall Street Journal* quote "experts" whose comments focus almost entirely on the outlook for the next day, week, or month.

Fortunately for those of us who don't want to spend our evenings and weekends poring over stock-market minutiae and arcana, market timing is nonsense. No one can predict what the stock market will do next week, next month, or next year. John Maynard Keynes, the eminent economist, called stock-market forecasting the art of "anticipating what average opinion expects the average opinion to be."

The *Hulbert Financial Digest*, one of our favorite publications, tracks the statistical record of recommendations by fifty leading investment newsletters, nearly all of which preach market timing.

*Hulbert* notes, among other things, the average "market exposure" recommended by these newsletters. Here's an example of their market-timing skill: On July 31, 1984, these eminent and expensive newsletters were recommending market exposure, on average, of 49 percent, the lowest level in a year. In other words, they were telling their readers to keep 51 percent of their assets in cash, only 49 percent in stocks. On August 1, the very next day, the Dow Jones Industrial Average jumped nineteen points. It leaped another thirty-one points on August 2 and added thirty-six points on August 3.

So much for calling stock-market turns, up or down. However, if history is any guide, we can count on stocks to grow in value over the long haul (see Lesson 20). The key to consistent profits from stocks is to buy for the long term and ride out the cycles. Historically, over any period of eight years or more, stocks have proved to be a superb investment. But the shorter the time you stay in the market, the more likely you are to lose money.

James B. Cloonan, president of the American Association of Individual Investors, surveyed the performance of the Standard & Poor's 500 stocks over the half-century from 1934 through 1983 (the Standard & Poor's 500 is a broad cross section of the stock market). Here's what Cloonan found out:

> If you had told your broker to buy the whole market at noon each day and sell it at noon the next day, you'd have taken a loss just under half the time. If you'd bought at the beginning of each year and sold at the end of each year, you'd have had a loss sixteen times in fifty years. If you bought at the beginning of each year and sold after five years, you would have lost only three times. If you bought every year and sold after eight years, you'd have never had a loss—not once in fifty years.

Cloonan is not working from secret statistics; the financial community is well aware that the stock market's record is very good for the long run and very iffy for the short. Nevertheless, the vast majority of stock market commentary and advice focuses on the immediate outlook, and millions of investors are conditioned to buy and sell in search of short-term profits. This defies logic, until you stop to think that brokers make money on transactions; advisers on time devoted to your account; and periodicals on advertising and circulation, which multiply according to frequency of publication. A more consistent and less frenetic approach benefits the investor, at the expense of those who trade stocks and peddle advice. If you buy stocks through mutual funds, you'll lessen your risks further and insulate yourself from the siren calls of stockbrokers.

A few stock-market professionals are brave enough to admit that they can't tell when the stock market will go up or down. One is John C. Burney, president of the Burney Company, a professional money management firm in Falls Church, Virginia. Over the past  decade, portfolios managed by Burney have achieved an average annual gain of 25.6 percent. When it comes to market timing and other sophisticated strategies, Burney has this to say: "We stay fully invested in stocks at all times. No one has yet been able to consistently predict what the market will do, so we don't even try. People say that 'buy and hold' is an obsolete strategy. Well, we buy and hold. On average, we hold a stock close to three years. Some stocks we've held for six to eight years."

Professionals like Burney have the time, knowledge, and incentive to study individual stocks, day in and day out. Most of us don't know how and don't want to spend the time anyway. Mutual funds were made for investors like us and for a strategy of long-term investing. In Lesson 21, we describe the unique advantages of mutual funds and tell you how to pick one or more that fit your objectives while offering records of consistent success.

# LESSON 20

## *Don't Be Afraid of Stocks— They Pay Off*

If you want your savings to grow into a comfortable nest egg, you should invest in stocks, using mutual funds. Stocks have an undeserved reputation for volatile risk. For the prudent, long-range investor, stocks are a steady and profitable investment. History proves it.

CDA Investment Technologies, Inc., an advisory firm, keeps a running tabulation of the comparative performance of various kinds of investments, assuming reinvestment of dividends and interest. For stocks, CDA uses the Standard & Poor's (S&P) 500; for bonds, it uses an index kept by Salomon Brothers, a big Wall Street investment company. (CDA Investment Technologies, Inc., can be reached at 11501 Georgia Ave., Silver Spring, MD 20902.)

Let's look first at the very long haul—sixty years, 1926 through 1985, covering the Great Depression, World War II, the postwar boom, the inflation binge that cooked the stock market in the 1970s, and the bull markets of recent years. Over all those turbulent eras, stocks yielded an average compound annual return of 9.8 percent, compared with 4.8 percent for corporate bonds, 4.2 percent for government bonds, and 3.4 percent for Treasury bills (often called "T-bills" for short). On average, the Consumer Price Index (CPI) rose by 3.1 percent a year.

The table on the top of the next page shows the average compound annual returns through 1985 for other time periods. For the five-year and one-year periods, note the effect of the unprecedented and extraordinary bull market that boosted bond prices so sharply.

Salomon Brothers tabulates a more extensive and somewhat more exotic index. This one includes collectibles—stamps, coins, old masters' paintings, Chinese ceramics. It also includes tangibles such as gold, silver, oil, and U.S. farmland. Most of these items are

AVERAGE COMPOUND ANNUAL RETURNS THROUGH 1985
(as tabulated by CDA Investment Technologies)

|                  | 60 years | 25 years | 10 years | 5 years | 1 year (1985) |
|------------------|----------|----------|----------|---------|---------------|
| Stocks           | 9.8%     | 9.5%     | 14.2%    | 14.6%   | 31.7%         |
| Corporate bonds  | 4.8      | 6.1      | 9.8      | 17.9    | 30.1          |
| Government bonds | 4.2      | 5.6      | 9.6      | 17.1    | 31.5          |
| T-bills          | 3.4      | 6.5      | 9.0      | 10.2    | 7.3           |
| CPI              | 3.1      | 5.3      | 7.0      | 4.8     | 3.8           |

AVERAGE COMPOUND ANNUAL RETURNS THROUGH
JUNE 1, 1985
(as tabulated by Salomon Brothers)

|                  | 15 years | 10 years | 5 years | 1 year |
|------------------|----------|----------|---------|--------|
| Stocks           | 8.5%     | 10.4%    | 15.2%   | 28.7%  |
| Bonds            | 8.7      | 9.3      | 13.2    | 42.9   |
| T-bills          | 9.1      | 10       | 12      | 9.5    |
| CPI              | 7.1      | 7.3      | 5.7     | 3.7    |
| Oil              | 19.7     | 8        | −5.4    | −4.5   |
| U.S. coins       | 17.7     | 20.4     | 0.1     | 11.5   |
| Gold             | 15.5     | 6.9      | −11     | −20.3  |
| Chinese ceramics | 14.3     | 17.1     | 1       | 5.9    |
| Stamps           | 14.1     | 14.5     | 0.1     | −9.6   |
| Diamonds         | 10.4     | 9.5      | 1.2     | 0      |
| Old masters      | 9.1      | 10.7     | 1.5     | 13.6   |
| Silver           | 8.7      | 3.5      | −15.9   | −34.3  |
| U.S. farmland    | 8.5      | 6.9      | −1.7    | −10    |
| Housing          | 8.2      | 7.9      | 4.3     | 2.5    |
| Foreign exchange | 2        | −0.6     | −7.9    | −11.3  |

beyond the reach of small investors, but the comparative figures are interesting.

The table above shows the compound annual rates of return, as tabulated by Salomon Brothers. For stocks, bonds, and T-bills, the dividends and interest are reinvested. This index figures years from June 1 to May 31 rather than using calendar years. For that reason and a few other technical differences, the figures don't precisely jibe with those of CDA Investment Technologies. The figures shown are through June 1, 1985.

As you can see, virtually all of these investments have performed moderately well over the fifteen-year period. Stocks, bonds, Treasury bills, and housing have been among the stablest investments. The most wildly fluctuating investments have been items that many people mistakenly assume to be immune to economic vagaries—gold, stamps, farmland—although they, too, have gained value over the long term.

Collectibles such as stamps, coins, Chinese ceramics, and old masters' paintings make superb investments for truly knowledgeable collectors who devote a great deal of time to them. But they are a trap for the uninformed. We couldn't tell a bogus Rembrandt from a real one, and we doubt that you could, either. Even if we could, we wouldn't have the slightest idea what one might be worth.

As investments, collectibles have another drawback, according to people who own them. Most people who collect stamps or coins or old masters do so out of true love. Few collect strictly to make money. So even the wisest collector is unlikely to cash in his profits, although he may sense that this is just the right time to do so. Sell his Rembrandt? Not on your life!

If you do decide to sell a valuable painting or coin or stamp, you often can't get the price you want—even if a dozen experts tell you that it's a fair price. You may face the choice of selling at a discount now or waiting months until a more generous buyer comes along. Another factor: Dealers mark up collectibles by a fat percentage. When you buy, you pay the marked-up retail price. When you sell— assuming you sell through a dealer—you get the marked-down wholesale price.

You may grow a little fond of a mutual fund, but you won't hang it on your wall. Chances are when the time comes, you can sell it, and enjoy your profit, without mourning the loss. You pay little or no commission to buy or to sell.

Here's another factor in favor of stocks. Both CDA Investment Technologies and Salomon Brothers base their figures for stocks on the Standard & Poor's 500, a cross-section list made up of large, widely held companies. By choosing good mutual funds, you can beat the S&P 500.

Buy art and other collectibles to enhance your pleasure. Buy mutual funds to enhance your security.

# The Very Best Mutual Funds and Why You Should Invest in Them to Build Your Nest Egg

Mutual funds provide the cornerstone of investment success for the smart money manager. A good mutual fund is a superb and sophisticated investment, yet it requires very little time and entails limited risk. You can easily choose funds with consistently good records and just as easily switch from one fund to another. You can choose among funds that produce growth and funds that produce income, and, in every category, you can pick established winners.

The case for mutual funds is so overwhelming that it is hard to understand why so many investors prefer to pick their own stocks. Thanks to publications that meticulously track the performance of hundreds of mutual funds, casual investors can readily choose among fifteen or twenty funds that have soundly beaten the market, year in and year out. Mutual fund investing is investing made easy. It is tailor-made for our time-saving plan. Every investment lesson in this book dovetails with a careful and consistent strategy of mutual fund investing.

Some investors enjoy the thrill of the hunt and make a hobby of investment research. Picking individual stocks takes a lot of time and requires a lot of expertise. After all, individual investors, working in their spare time, have to compete with full-time investment professionals. If you want to limit the time that you spend on investments and other areas of family finance, forget individual stocks. Through mutual funds, you can invest collectively, intelligently, and conveniently.

When you invest in a mutual fund, your money is added to that of other investors and used to buy a portfolio of stocks or bonds, chosen and managed by full-time professionals. For example, Twentieth Century Select, headquartered in Kansas City and one of the mutual funds that we recommend, holds stocks in about seventy companies, spread among seventeen industries, from aerospace to waste disposal.

A diversified portfolio provides safety, but only a good manager achieves success. The average mutual fund performs about as well as the stock market as a whole. That's not bad: stocks have outperformed other investments over any long-range period going back to 1929. This lesson will show you how to pick funds that have soundly trounced the market averages.

Moreover, you can do it yourself, based entirely on the record. In mutual fund investing, there is no such thing as a hot tip, and there is no reason to lean on a broker for advice. If you do, your broker will probably steer you to a "load" fund—one that imposes a sales commission, typically about 8.5 percent of your investment. Among the mutual funds with the best records, a majority are sold by mail, bypassing brokers. Most of these charge no sales commission and thus are called "no-loads." A few charge loads of 2 or 3 percent of the total investment. Most funds, load or no-load, charge an annual administrative fee of about 1 percent.

As a mutual fund investor, you can invest a little money or a lot, and you never have to call a broker or endorse a dividend check; at your option, dividends and capital gains distributions can be automatically reinvested. You can easily keep track of how well your fund is performing and how its performance compares with that of other funds.

Moreover, you can easily switch from one fund to another. Big investment companies like Dreyfus ([800] 645-6561), Fidelity ([800] 544-6666), Price ([800] 638-5660), and Vanguard ([800] 662-7447) manage a number of mutual funds and let you switch from one to another by telephone. With a letter, you can switch your money from a fund managed by one company to a fund managed by another.

Many investors use this switching privilege to move their money from a stock fund to a money market fund or vice versa. Before moving out of a stock fund, though, consider whether you would incur a taxable gain; to the Internal Revenue Service, a switch is a sale.

All mutual funds try to make money, but they do so in different ways. Among mutual funds that buy stocks, some strive for maximum growth, ignoring dividends and taking risks. Others seek long-term growth in value, using a more conservative approach. "Growth and income" funds choose stocks that pay good dividends and also offer prospects for growth. Other funds specialize in the stocks of small companies or overseas firms, or they mix bonds with stocks. Still other mutual funds invest for income; we discuss those funds in Lesson 27.

Mutual fund categories are proliferating, because the industry is hotly competitive and the companies that offer mutual funds are always looking for a new way to catch the investor's eye—and dollar. The latest rage is "sector investing"—funds that specialize in particular industries, such as science and technology, financial services, health care, energy, leisure and entertainment, utilities, defense and aerospace, and gold mining. Sector funds tend to be more speculative because they narrow your diversification. But some have performed spectacularly during their relatively brief existence.

Investment managers can make a good case for any approach, from the broad scope of a general fund to the narrow limits of a sector fund. In fact, some funds in every category have performed very well, and some in every category have fallen flat. Even casual investors tend to harbor investment philosophies, and the variety of successful mutual funds lets you indulge your beliefs without taking foolish risks.

For example, many investors look askance at dividends, believing that a company should invest its profits in research or new facilities rather than paying that money to shareholders. Those who see the arms race continuing might put their dollars in defense and aerospace funds, while those who see America becoming a playground might prefer funds that specialize in the leisure and entertainment industries.

Most investors are better off with funds that are more general in their approach. But picking the right fund is more important than picking the right category.

To hedge their bets, some investors spread their money among funds in several categories. That's prudent to a degree, but the more funds you choose, the more likely it is that you will "buy the market"—diversify so much that your overall portfolio tracks the stock market rather than beating it.

You can get enough diversification with one or two or three mutual funds, chosen carefully on the basis of their performance and their probable effect on your income tax. Mutual funds that pay high interest or dividends fit Individual Retirement Accounts

(IRAs) and other retirement accounts because dividends and interest within a retirement account are not taxed until withdrawn. Funds that concentrate on growth work better outside retirement accounts. (Within an IRA, you pay no income tax on dividends, interest, or capital gains. But when you start withdrawing money from your IRA, you pay income tax on every dollar withdrawn, no matter its source.)

Now how do you choose the best mutual funds? And after investing in one or more funds, how do you keep track of their performance, so you can tell whether it might be wise to switch to better funds?

Based on performance through September 1986, the accompanying table shows fifteen mutual funds we particularly recommend. They have rung up consistently superior results. By "performance," we mean the investor's actual profit or loss—change in the market value of each share, plus dividends. These figures assume that all dividends are reinvested in the fund. The figures are provided by the publishers of *Schabacker's Mutual Fund Quarterly Performance Review* (the address is given later in this lesson), our favorite mutual fund newsletter. Much as we like mutual funds, these in particular, we must caution you not to get carried away by the performance figures for the past twelve months. That was a spectacular period for the stock market. But it's not realistic to expect one wild bull-market year after another.

All these funds are sold by telephone and mail, bypassing brokers. Except where noted, funds are no-loads, meaning that you pay no sales commission.

Before buying, you might want to check more current results. Even after buying, we recommend that you check twice a year, to make sure your funds are still performing well. We have a shortcut way of checking mutual fund investments: at least once a year, send a check for $25 to Schabacker Investment Management, 8943 Shady Grove Court, Gaithersburg, Maryland 20877, and order the current issue of *Schabacker's Mutual Fund Quarterly Performance Review.* It's published in late January, April, July, and October.

Check the fund rankings and performance for the past year and—more important—for the past five years and ten years. Any fund might shine for a month or a year. The best funds are those that weather good and bad market periods and rank high for long-term performance. If your fund has fallen in the rankings and you see a long-term performer that you prefer, switch; it's your money.

## FIFTEEN RECOMMENDED MUTUAL FUNDS

| | Performance through September 1986 for the past | | |
| --- | --- | --- | --- |
| | 1 year | 5 years | 10 years |
| FUNDS SEEKING CAPITAL GAINS WITH AGGRESSIVE APPROACH—HIGHEST RISK | | | |
| Weingarten Equity Fund<br>331 Madison Avenue<br>New York, New York 10017<br>([800] 231-0803;<br>in Texas [800] 392-9681) | up 38% | up 179% | up 681% |
| Evergreen Fund<br>550 Mamaroneck Avenue<br>Harrison, New York 10528<br>([800] 635-0003 or [914] 698-5711) | up 30% | up 165% | up 901% |
| Tudor Fund<br>1 New York Plaza<br>30th Floor<br>New York, New York 10004<br>([800] 223-3332 or [212] 908-9582) | up 29% | up 180% | up 572% |
| FUNDS SEEKING CAPITAL GAINS WITH MORE CONSERVATIVE APPROACH—MODERATE RISK | | | |
| Fidelity Magellan (3% load)<br>Fidelity Investments<br>82 Devonshire Street<br>Boston, Massachusetts 02109<br>([800] 544-6666 or [617] 523-1919) | up 44% | up 290% | up 1,617% |
| Twentieth Century Select<br>Twentieth Century Investors<br>P.O. Box 200<br>Kansas City, Missouri 64141<br>([800] 345-2021 or [816] 531-5575) | up 35% | up 187% | up 1,002% |
| Nicholas Fund<br>312 E. Wisconsin Avenue<br>Milwaukee, Wisconsin 53202<br>([414] 272-6133) | up 19% | up 187% | up 749% |
| Mutual Shares<br>Mutual Shares Corp.<br>26 Broadway<br>New York, New York 10004<br>([800] 457-0211 or [212] 908-4047) | up 20% | up 170% | up 593% |
| FUNDS SEEKING INCOME WITH MODERATE GROWTH—LOWEST RISK | | | |
| Fidelity Equity Income (2% load)<br>Fidelity Investments<br>82 Devonshire Street<br>Boston, Massachusetts 02109<br>([800] 544-6666 or [617] 523-1919) | up 24% | up 197% | up 559% |

## FIFTEEN RECOMMENDED MUTUAL FUNDS (continued)

| | Performance through September 1986 for the past | | |
|---|---|---|---|
| | 1 year | 5 years | 10 years |
| Evergreen Total Return<br>Evergreen Funds<br>550 Mamaroneck Avenue<br>Harrison, New York 10528<br>([800] 635-0003 or [914] 698-5711) | up 28% | up 212% | less than ten years old |
| Financial Programs Industrial Income<br>P.O. Box 2040<br>Englewood, Colorado 80201<br>([800] 525-8085; in Colorado [800] 332-7388) | up 32% | up 179% | up 340% |
| Vanguard Wellesley<br>Vanguard Group<br>Valley Forge, Pennsylvania 19482<br>([800] 662-7447 or [215] 648-6000) | up 25% | up 169% | up 232% |
| SECTOR FUNDS | | | |
| Fidelity Health Care (2% load)<br>Fidelity Investments<br>82 Devonshire Street<br>Boston, Massachusetts 02109<br>([800] 544-6666 or [617] 523-1919) | up 40% | up 244% | less than ten years old |
| Fidelity Leisure (2% load)<br>Fidelity Investments<br>82 Devonshire Street<br>Boston, Massachusetts 02109<br>([800] 544-6666 or [617] 523-1919) | up 40% | | less than five years old |
| Fidelity Utilities (2% load)<br>Fidelity Investments<br>82 Devonshire Street<br>Boston, Massachusetts 02109<br>([800] 544-6666 or [617] 523-1919) | up 43% | | less than five years old |
| Scudder International<br>Scudder Fund Distributors<br>175 Federal Street<br>Boston, Massachusetts 02110<br>([800] 453-3305 or [617] 426-8300) | up 63% | up 194% | up 402% |

In late August, start watching the newsstands for the annual mutual funds issue of *Forbes* magazine. In 1985, the mutual funds issue was dated September 16; in 1986, it was dated September 8. The cover always calls attention to the mutual fund rankings, so you'll readily recognize the issue when it appears on newsstands.

*Forbes* gives each mutual fund a letter grade—from A to F, like a report card—for its performance in "up" markets and another grade for its performance in "down" markets. Funds that rank A or B in both categories are listed in a special "honor roll."

If you stick with mutual funds that make the *Forbes* honor roll in August or September and also rank high in a winter or spring issue of *Schabacker's*, you'll have a winning investment program. It'll cost you $28.50 a year, tax-deductible—$25 for *Schabacker's*, $3.50 for *Forbes*, barring price increases. The whole process won't take more than an hour or two in the spring and another hour or two in the fall. For $28.50 and three or four hours, you'll have a genuinely sophisticated and reliable investment program—assuming, of course, that you follow the other investment lessons in this book, none of which is complicated.

Avoid brokers. Make your own decisions. Buy mutual funds that invest in stocks and don't try to predict the course of the stock market. Stick to a regular investing schedule so you can take advantage of dollar-cost averaging (discussed in the following lesson) and so you'll benefit from the stock market's erratic but reliable long-term gains. Don't let greed get the best of your judgment. Avoid all investments that you don't understand.

If you follow these simple lessons, you'll save time, spare yourself a lot of worry, and build a sizable nest egg. It sure beats long evenings with *Investor's Daily* and other such publications. And it sure beats losing money on swindles or fads or long shots.

Mutual fund investors don't shine when party talk turns to investments. Someone is likely to boast of buying Digital Switch at two bucks a share or doubling her money on a beach house. But these braggarts don't tell you about their losses. Anyway, while they study and worry about their stocks and real estate, you can spend your time on activities more to your taste. Chances are, your plain vanilla mutual fund will still be earning a good return when their latest venture takes a dive.

# LESSON 22

## *An Investment Program So Simple That It Works: Dollar-Cost Averaging*

By following a simple program of regular investing called dollar-cost averaging, you can outpace the stock market and outperform the investment professionals.

As an investment strategy, dollar-cost averaging is so straightforward and simple that it puts Wall Street to sleep. It isn't sexy, it isn't new, and it won't give you much in the way of sparkling conversation at cocktail parties. But it has three redeeming features: It works. It requires very little time or effort. And it eliminates the anxiety that goes with trickier, more speculative investment schemes.

Dollar-cost averaging dovetails perfectly with the use of mutual funds, employing the strategy that we recommended in Lesson 21. To use dollar-cost averaging, you carefully choose a mutual fund or two and invest a regular fixed amount at regular fixed intervals. For simplicity, we recommend that you do it every January and June. For example, if you've decided that you can invest $2,000 during the year, invest $1,000 in January and the other $1,000 in June.

You may want to set your own schedule. But whatever schedule you decide upon, and whatever amount you can afford to invest every year, stick to it over the course of at least one entire business cycle. Four or five years works out about right. Never skip a payment or vary your schedule.

With dollar-cost averaging, you don't have to anguish over when or how much to invest. For example, as we write this, the Dow Jones Industrial Average settled around 1,850 after soaring to a record high above 1,900. Will it climb to 1,900 again, or perhaps to 2,000? Or will it drift down? Should you invest now or wait? Dollar-cost averaging eliminates that kind of guesswork. Whether the market is high or low, you stick to your schedule.

## DOLLAR-COST AVERAGING: EXAMPLE

| Year | Amount of purchase | Price per share | Number of shares purchased |
|------|--------------------|-----------------|----------------------------|
| 1 | $1,000 | $10 | 100 |
| 2 | 1,000 | 20 | 50 |
| 3 | 1,000 | 15 | 66.67 |
| 4 | 1,000 | 21 | 47.62 |
| TOTAL | 4,000 | | 264.29 |

It works because with dollar-cost averaging, you're opting out of market timing—the risky game that makes the blood race and the Dow rise and fall like a rowboat in a hurricane.

Arithmetic works in favor of dollar-cost averaging. Strange as it may seem, your average cost per share comes out to less than the average price you paid. The accompanying table shows an example, provided for us by Fidelity Investments. Say you invest $1,000 at the start of each year for four years, and the per-share price varies as in the table. In four years, you have bought 264.29 shares for $4,000, so your average cost was $15.13 per share. But the average price—$10 plus $20 plus $15 plus $21, divided by four (the number of purchases you made)—was $16.50. Dollar-cost averaging has saved you $1.37 a share, or $362.08 altogether. More important, of course, it has vaccinated you against the risks of market-timing fever.

Dollar-cost averaging is further enhanced by reinvestment of dividends. Nearly all mutual funds offer automatic dividend-reinvestment plans. That's one of many reasons we favor mutual funds.

To many investors, dollar-cost averaging sounds suspiciously like something their mothers would advocate, while wagging one finger and pointing at a piggy bank with the other. Small savings, big bother. Go away, Mom.

In fact, you can build up quite a nest egg. Say you invest $2,000 at the start of every year, and your account earns 10 percent a year, compounded annually. Look at the table on the next page to see how your account builds.

Of course, dollar-cost averaging would be suicidal if your investment regularly declined in value. It is not an excuse for sticking with a losing mutual fund; you can switch to a more promising fund without losing a step in your schedule. But dollar-cost averaging imposes a useful discipline. It does not let you sell out when you are feeling pessimistic or splurge when you are feeling optimistic.

## ACCOUNT GROWTH: EXAMPLE

|                | Total amount | |
|----------------|----------|----------|
|                | Invested | Value |
| After 10 years | $20,000  | $ 35,062 |
| After 20 years | 40,000   | 126,005 |
| After 25 years | 50,000   | 216,364 |
| After 40 years | 80,000   | 973,704 |

It also helps you resist the advice of any number of experts who argue passionately that their "buy" and "sell" signals will make you rich by telling you just when to get into the market and just when to get out.

Given the stock market's long-term success and its penchant for short-term gyrations, you might expect most investors to ride out the ups and downs by using a dispassionate, long-term strategy such as dollar-cost averaging. But they do not. Every year, about three-fifths of the outstanding shares of stock in U.S. corporations changes hands. James Tobin, a Yale economist who served on the Council of Economic Advisers under President Kennedy, notes that no other country churns stocks at such a rate. Japan ranks second at 35 percent, Germany third at 24 percent, and Great Britain fourth at 16 percent.

Curiously, the busiest churners are not nervous little investors but big institutions—particularly pension funds. It's important to understand why, because it takes a strong constitution and conviction to stick with dollar-cost averaging in the face of massive market moves triggered by investment professionals.

Pension funds are far and away the largest owners of stocks and bonds in the United States, and their share is growing. Many corporate and union pension funds hire investment firms—professional money managers—to invest and manage these growing pools of wealth. Scores of investment firms compete for this lucrative business.

Corporations and unions naturally choose investment firms that achieve the best results. Federal law requires pension funds to maintain prudent standards, so corporations tend to drop money managers whose performance lags.

As a result, professional money managers find themselves driven into short-term market strategies. They have become the ultimate "market timers," jumping in and out of the stock market lest a more consistent strategy leave them looking bad for the past quarter—a performance that could cost them the business, however sound their strategy may be for the long term.

Because these institutional investors are always looking over their shoulders at each other, they tend to follow one another pell-mell. In this atmosphere, the courage of a manager's convictions is usually trampled by the herd instinct. When the stock market set records in late 1985 and 1986, it was not because a new wisdom revealed itself to Wall Street but because the market looked to be moving up and the pros, who had been holding a good deal of their pension-fund money in cash, didn't want to be left at the gate.

That's one reason the stock market sometimes gyrates so much in a single day or a week—the herd instinct overcomes rational judgment. Many pension fund managers program their computers to automatically sell stocks any time the market declines by a certain amount, and to buy stocks any time the market rises by a certain amount. This is money management by band wagon, and it has nothing to do with prudent long-range investing. But you don't have to go along with this ulcer-causing lunacy. You'll be better off hum-drumming along with dollar-cost averaging. If you doubt that regular investing in a good mutual fund will make you enough money, look again at the gains chalked up during the past decade by the mutual funds that we recommended in Lesson 21.

You do not need to beat other investors every three months; your goal is to earn more, over time, than you could earn by simply putting your savings in an insured money market account or a money market mutual fund. If you choose good mutual funds, following our suggestions in Lesson 21, and stick with a strategy of regular investing, you will armor yourself against short-term market swings while sharing in long-term market gains.

But will the stock market's future be as bright as its past? We think it will, thanks largely to—of all institutions—the pension funds. We all read from time to time that Americans don't save enough of their income, but these figures ignore the massive savings accumulating in pension funds.

Pension funds now manage more than $2 trillion in assets. That figure grew by more than $200 billion in 1985 and by even more in 1986. Before the end of the century, pension-fund assets will reach

$10 trillion, according to projections by the Employee Benefit Research Institute, a nonprofit research organization.

How much is $10 trillion? It looks like this! $10,000,000,000,000. It's more than triple the national debt. It's roughly five times the market value of all the shares of common stock listed on the New York Stock Exchange. It's about thirty-five times the value of all the mutual funds put together (not counting money market funds). And no matter how skittish and conservative the pension-fund managers may be, they have to invest that money somewhere.

In fact, a pension-fund manager has fewer choices than you have, as a small investor. The corporation has to come up with its regular pension-fund contribution every year, in good times and bad. The manager cannot put that money in oriental rugs or rare stamps or gold coins; those investments aren't practical when you're managing billions of dollars of other people's money and you have to generate enough income to cover thousands of monthly pension checks.

So the pension funds stick to paper investments—stocks, bonds, mortgages, insurance contracts, and cash equivalents such as Treasury bills. Fund managers churn their portfolios among those investments, making the stock market swing up and down. But stocks are the favorite investment of most pension-fund managers, for the same reason that we recommend them to you: historically, stocks produce superior returns.

Here's how the nation's two hundred largest pension funds had their money invested at the end of September 1985, according to *Pensions and Investment Age*, a trade publication:

|  | Percent invested |
| --- | --- |
| Stocks | 42% |
| Bonds | 33 |
| Cash equivalents | 9 |
| Mortgages and mortgage securities | 5 |
| Real estate | 4 |
| Insurance contracts | 4 |
| All other | 3 |

The growth of pension funds seems almost certain to gradually boost stock prices over time, however erratically.

Retirement accounts will help, too. The majority of IRA dollars have been going into banks and savings institutions, but the share going into stocks and mutual funds is growing fast. News accounts to the contrary, the new tax law did not kill IRAs (see Lesson 50).

The greater the demand, the more likely it is that stock prices will rise—again, with the usual ups and downs. The sensational bull market of late 1985 and 1986 was fueled largely by pension funds.

That's a long dissertation, but it's the foundation for the wise strategy of dollar-cost averaging. Mutual funds provide a convenient and diversified investment for dollar-cost averaging. You can invest small amounts, by mail, without paying any "load," or sales commission. By following Lesson 21, you can choose funds with superb records, and you can keep track of the funds you have chosen.

# LESSON 23

## *Mutual Fund Tax Tactics*

Outside a tax-sheltered retirement account, never buy a mutual fund just before it pays a dividend.

A mutual fund accumulates its earnings from dividends and growth and pays those earnings to shareholders on a regular basis. Some funds pay dividends four times a year, some twice a year, others just once a year.

As earnings accumulate, that cash is counted in the per-share price of the fund—the "net asset value," meaning the value of all the fund's holdings (stocks, cash, bonds) divided by the number of fund shares outstanding. When the dividend is paid, the net asset value of each share declines by the amount of the dividend. The fund has paid out that money. It's now in the pockets of shareholders.

Let's say you buy Fund X at $10 a share, and a week later it pays a dividend of 50 cents. The net asset value will drop by 50 cents, so the share you bought for $10 will be worth only $9.50. You'll have that 50 cents in the form of dividend income, fully taxable. That's called "buying a dividend."

Better to buy right after the dividend is paid. That way you get the shares for $9.50—ten bucks minus the 50-cent dividend. So you get more shares for your money. And since you haven't collected a dividend, you don't owe any tax.

When you call to inquire about a mutual fund, ask the dates of its regular dividend payouts. Time your investments accordingly—after dividends are paid, not before.

If and when you sell mutual fund shares, consider the effect on your income tax. Let's say the fund you bought hasn't lived up to expectations, and you want to switch to a fund with a better record, using the system recommended in Lesson 21. If you have lost money on your investment, consider selling before year's end, so you can take advantage of the loss on your current income tax. Up to $3,000 a year in net capital losses can be deducted in full on your tax return.

If you show a profit, reverse the strategy. By waiting until the following year, you'll postpone the tax on your profit.

During the year, a mutual fund buys and sells shares within its portfolio. You'll have to pay tax on your share of the fund's own capital gains (the more the merrier, since you want your fund to make money). But when it comes to selling fund shares, use losses to reduce your income tax, and postpone gains to postpone income tax.

# LESSON 24

## *Where to Invest Small Amounts*

Want to buy a chunk of Wall Street for five bucks? We've got just the right investment—in fact, one of the very best mutual funds.

Few banks pay competitive money market interest on small accounts, and most mutual funds require an initial investment of $500 to $2,000. But Twentieth Century Investors, a well-managed mutual fund company in Kansas City, will take an account of any size. "You mean you'll open an account if I send you one buck?" we asked. "Yep," they said. It sounded as if they get asked that question a lot.

Twentieth Century offers a money market mutual fund, four equity funds (mutual funds that invest in stocks), and one bond fund. All its funds are no-loads, meaning that you buy and sell by mail order, paying no commission.

You'll find Twentieth Century Select, an equity fund, among the consistent winners that we recommend in Lesson 21. Twentieth Century U.S. Government Fund is a conservative short-term bond fund. Twentieth Century Cash Reserve, the money market fund, pays interest rates just as competitive as funds or banks that turn up their noses at accounts of less than a thousand or two thousand bucks.

The variety makes Twentieth Century an ideal mutual fund "family" for a balanced investment program. Other mutual fund "families" such as Fidelity and Vanguard are just as good, but only Twentieth Century will open a really tiny account. It's ideal for starting a child on an investment program. We know a part-time housekeeper who contributes $20 a month to an Individual Retirement Account (IRA) with Twentieth Century (the firm charges $10 a year to manage an IRA account). You can get the details by phoning (816) 531-5575 or writing to Twentieth Century Investors, 605 West 47th Street, Kansas City, Missouri 64112.

You cannot write checks on Twentieth Century Cash Reserve. Most money market mutual funds that offer checking account privileges won't take an account smaller than $1,000 or $2,000. One will: First Trust Funds, 110 North Franklin Street, Chicago, Illinois 60606 ([800] 621-4770). First Trust will open a money market account for a buck. But you can't write a check on the fund for less than $100, so you don't get checks until your balance reaches $100. The checks are free. First Trust offers a regular money market fund, another that buys only U.S. government money market securities, and a third that specializes in tax-free money market investments. Take your choice.

# LESSON 25

## *Investments to Avoid*

For your own financial safety, never, ever trade options, warrants, commodities, or futures of any kind. Stay away from real estate and oil and gas limited partnerships, cattle-feeding deals, and equipment-leasing operations. Don't buy Ginnie Maes. We even recommend that you avoid individual stocks and bonds.

It sounds smart to say that you're dabbling in commodities or Treasury bond futures. But it's about as smart as swimming with sharks.

We'd advise against these investments even for people with plenty of money and plenty of time to devote to their portfolios. Comedian George Burns, ninety years old and surely not short of cash, recently was asked if he ever traded futures. His reply: "Me buy futures? I don't even buy green bananas!"

For a part-time investor, tricky and complicated investments like the ones listed above are worse than foolish. At their best, options, warrants, commodities, and futures require microscopic care and precise timing. For anyone but a professional, risking money in such enterprises is like flying an airplane without lessons.

Years ago, *Money* magazine quoted an authority who said you could be sure of only three things if you traded options: "You will lose most or all of your money, you will lose most or all of your money, and you will lose most or all of your money."

When you buy an option "call," you shell out cash for the right to buy one hundred shares of a certain stock at a certain price any-time during a set period—usually, the next three months. When you buy an option "put," you shell out cash for the right to sell one hundred shares at a certain price. A warrant is a similar right to buy at a set price but covers only one share and usually lasts for a longer period.

Commodities and other futures work on the same principle: investors gamble that they can outguess the experts in predicting short-term swings in the price of Treasury bonds, hog bellies, wheat, various stock-market indexes—you name it.

The lure is like that of roulette: you don't have to bet much, and if you bet right, you can win big. The reality is that you're much more likely to lose.

Today, you can even buy futures on the Consumer Price Index. In other words, you can lay down a bet—legally, in the form of a futures contract—on the rate of inflation a year from now. Phillip Cagan, an economist at Columbia University, has studied inflation forecasts in detail and comes to just the conclusion you would expect: no one can predict the course of inflation more than a few months ahead. The same is true of everything else on which futures or options are bought and sold. It's a guess, a hunch, an absolute gamble, no better or worse than picking a number on a roulette wheel.

Brokers will sing you a different song. They'll tell you that their firm has an exclusive hookup with a couple of guys with an impeccable record of beating the options market or the commodities market or whatever. If you believe that, you'll believe the guy who claims a winning system at roulette.

Although the new tax law has dried up many tax-shelter limited partnerships, salespeople still hawk partnerships in real estate that are designed to produce income, and partnerships in oil and gas that are alleged to reduce your taxes and yield an eventual gain. It's almost impossible to buy into one of these without putting your faith in a company and a venture about which you know very little.

We've read prospectuses for various partnerships, and we've never seen one that tells you precisely how much of your money would get swallowed up in fees and commissions. No wonder; sponsors sometimes siphon off as much as 30 percent. Most partnerships commit you to invest a certain amount every year for several years. And your investment is illiquid. That means you can't change your mind and sell it. Or if you do, you'll sell at a steep loss, even if the partnership is proceeding profitably.

Real estate and oil partnerships are the most common, but cattle-feeding and equipment-leasing deals fall into the same category. These are investments that may work for a knowledgeable professional but are not appropriate for a part-time investor.

For example, we recently got a mailer from a cattle company in Amarillo, Texas, telling us that this would be a fine time to buy into cattle feeding to profit from rising cattle prices. Well, maybe so, but how are we supposed to know what will happen to cattle prices? Better to stick with proven, straightforward investments that you understand. If you're looking for a tax-sheltered investment, consider buying a house or condo and renting it out. We describe that investment in Lesson 34. For tax-free income, consider municipal bonds (Lesson 27) or single-premium whole life insurance (Lesson 28).

Ginnie Maes seem to be hot these days. We sometimes wonder how radio and television stations would fill their commercial time without brokers hawking the "wonderful returns" from GNMA trusts. But except for retirement accounts, Ginnie Maes are fiendishly complicated.

GNMA, or Ginnie Mae, stands for the Government National Mortgage Association, a federal agency that buys mortgages from banks and other lenders, batches them, and sells them to investment houses, which in turn break them into trust units. Brokers sell these units for as little as $1,000 each, charging a "load," or commission, of 3.5 percent.

Ginnie Mae mortgages are guaranteed by the government, and they do yield a percentage point or two more interest than Treasury bonds. Investors collect interest, and collect principal as the mortgages within the trust are paid off.

Trouble is, you never know when that will be. Typically, a unit trust bundles a batch of twenty-five-year mortgages. But most mortgages are paid off way before maturity, because mortgage borrowers sell their houses and move. In addition, as interest rates declined in late 1985 and throughout 1986, many borrowers closed out their old mortgages to refinance at lower interest rates. On average, GNMA mortgages are paid off in twelve or thirteen years. Even on the mortgages still outstanding, the borrowers pay some interest and some principal every month, just as you do on your home mortgage.

If you buy into a unit trust, every monthly check you get includes some interest and some return of principal. You don't know how much you'll get each month or how long the trust will last, and the statements reflecting the mixture of interest and principal are hard to fathom. A broker friend (yes, we do some slumming) told us about one unhappy GNMA customer: "I had a senior partner at one of the Big Eight accounting firms who couldn't figure out his statement."

Only in a retirement account such as an Individual Retirement

Account (IRA) is a Ginnie Mae trust practical, because the monthly payments will automatically be reinvested, and since the earnings aren't taxed, you don't have to sort out the difference between interest and principal payments. However, we prefer no-load mutual funds, some of which invest in mortgage securities. You buy shares rather than trust units, and as the fund receives principal payments, it reinvests the money in more mortgages. So you get regular interest, at reasonably high rates, without complication. These mortgage mutual funds are good, conservative, income-yielding investments, whether in a retirement account or outside one. Try Fidelity Mortgage Securities at (800) 544-6666 or Vanguard GNMA Portfolio at (800) 662-7447.

Our last no-no sermon has to do with individual stocks and bonds. We strongly recommend mutual funds for both kinds of investments.

Individual stocks can be lots of fun and provide lots of excitement. But picking winners is chancy at best. Anytime you get some information that might lead you to buy or sell a stock, you can be sure that pension funds and other big investors got the same information first, so the price of the stock already has risen or dropped before you have a chance to buy or sell.

Moreover, every investor needs a diversified portfolio. It costs a lot of money to buy a diversified portfolio on your own, and it takes a lot of time and expertise to pick the stocks in the first place and then to manage the portfolio. Why not hire a mutual fund manager who has the time and expertise, and who has proved her competence? We could write a book about investing in individual stocks, but it is not a strategy that fits the needs of a part-time investor. In fact, mutual funds, in our opinion, are sounder for nearly all investors. In investing, "sophistication" has nothing to do with complication. Sophisticated investors are investors who follow prudent and profitable strategies. Good mutual funds are profitable, and investing in them is prudent. You'll find winning funds listed in Lesson 21.

Individual bonds make even less sense, regardless of whether they're issued by the Treasury, a corporation, or—for tax-free interest—a city or state. Individual bonds are for big-shot investors with $100,000 or more to plunk down. Most bonds cost $5,000 each, and those are the little ones; big shots buy units of $100,000 or $1 million and get a discount.

When you buy a bond through a broker, you're not even told how much the broker pockets. Brokerage firms sell bonds from their own inventories and mark up the price when they sell to small investors. If you later want to sell the bond before it matures, the broker pays you a lower price, the better to set himself up for another profit when he resells that bond.

Besides, one or two bonds don't provide diversification. You leave yourself open to interest-rate swings and other risks. And while issuers rarely default on bonds, it can happen. If you don't believe this, talk to any of the thousands of investors who bought bonds some years ago in the Washington Public Power System, which became known as WHOOPS when the bonds went bad and many people lost heavily.

By buying shares in one of the no-load bond funds that we recommend in Lesson 27, you can enjoy bond income, taxable or tax-free, with a diversified and professionally managed portfolio. It's the better and easier way. Treasury bonds, of course, are guaranteed, and you can buy them directly from the Treasury Department or a Federal Reserve bank. But that's a time-consuming process. If you like the safety of Treasuries, buy them through a mutual fund that buys only Treasury bonds.


None of this is bad news for the part-time investor. It means that you can safely ignore every news story, magazine article, and conversation about a broad array of investments. These investments range from foolish to risky to needlessly complicated and occupy the time (and money) of a lot of people. You can apply that time to your tennis game or your garden.

# *Balancing Your Investments*

Keep enough cash on hand to handle emergencies. To build a nest egg, invest for long-term gain.

This whole investment process is a bit of a balancing act, and you have to weigh your own inclinations, and weaknesses, in deciding how to apportion your money. The standard advice is to keep enough cash on hand (in a money market account) to support you for six months. But if you observe that rule, you may have nothing left to invest. Six months' worth of living costs comes to a whole lot of money. Moreover, the more cash on hand, the more you spend.

On the other hand, you don't want to leave yourself short of cash, and forced to sell mutual fund shares or real estate. The stock and real estate markets are cyclical, and you want to guard against a cash shortage that might force you to sell during a down cycle, when prices are low. The key to successful investing, in mutual funds or real estate, is to invest for the long term. If and when you cash in those assets, you want to do it at your convenience, when the price is right.

Work out a formula that maintains enough cash but doesn't cripple your investment program. You can get started with help from Lessons 8 and 22.

It's wise to balance your investments, with some aimed for growth—a category that carries risk—and some pegged to earn high interest or dividends. If you can afford to re-invest the interest or dividends, so much the better.

When investing, always pay attention to the federal income tax. Although capital gains no longer get preferential tax treatment, it is still true that you pay no federal income tax on the growing value of your investments until you cash them in. So a growth mutual fund or a house that grows in value retains an element of tax preference.

So does an IRA contribution. To be sure, the new tax law limits the deductibility of IRA contributions. But most Americans still qualify for the deduction; see Lesson 50 to find out where you stand. Even if you can no longer deduct your $2,000 IRA contribution, the interest or dividends earned by your IRA will continue to accumulate free of income tax until you withdraw the money, usually after age 59½. So investments that pay high yield make sense for an IRA and for any other tax-sheltered retirement account, such as a 401(k) or a Keogh.

By now you know the logical rule of thumb: If you have $4,000 to invest and qualify for an IRA deduction, put $2,000 in your IRA, pegged to earn high yield, and $2,000 outside your IRA, pegged for growth. Let both investment accounts grow into a nest egg. For income to spend, invest in one of the bond funds recommended in Lesson 27.

Here's a sample breakdown of how you might invest $8,000:

- *IRA*—$2,000 in Fidelity Equity Income Fund ([800] 544-6666), which earns a good dividend yield and also provides growth in value. For a more conservative approach geared entirely to high yield, Price New Income Fund ([800] 638-5660), or a certificate of deposit (see Lesson 27).
- *Outside IRA*—For maximum growth, $2,000 in Evergreen Fund ([800] 636-0003). For an investment that yields tax-free spending money, $2,000 in Vanguard Municipals Intermediate Term ([800] 662-7447). For cash, $2,000 in a high-yield money market fund.

In Lessons 21 and 27, you'll find more information about investing for growth and investing for income, with more funds listed. In Lesson 51, you'll find more help on investing your IRA money.

## *More Investment Strategies*

The right investments yield good income, save on taxes, and compound in value. You can balance one investment with another to achieve your financial goals.

 *To Do*

- Monthly budget
- Subscribe to *Tiered Rate Watch* (see page 119)
- If you have children, you can give them up to $10,000 per year without paying federal gift tax ($20,000 if you're married)
- Subscribe to Audit's Realty Stock Review if you are interested in Real Estate Investment Trusts (see page 135)
- You should have received your tax refund by May 30.

# *Investing for Income*

For income, buy high-yielding certificates of deposit (CDs) or mutual funds that hold short-term bonds. Stick to tax-free municipals unless your tax bracket is very low. Keep cash in an insured money market account or a money market mutual fund.

To save time, many people buy certificates of deposit from the handiest bank or savings institution. In extreme cases, a casual choice like that can cost you thousands of dollars. That's because some banks pay more interest than others. With the magic of compounding over a number of years, one or two percentage points of interest can amount to a lot of money.

Here's a quick, easy way to get the highest yields on insured money market accounts and CDs. Call (800) 447-0011 and order a subscription to *Tiered Rate Watch*, a monthly newsletter that lists the highest yields paid on federally insured CDs and money market accounts by banks and savings institutions throughout the country. (Or write *Tiered Rate Watch*, P.O. Drawer 145510, Coral Gables, FL 33114.) A one-year subscription costs $99; a three-month subscription costs $39. Publisher Paul Bauer and his staff survey about seven hundred institutions. Each issue of the six-page newsletter lists those paying the highest yields on money market accounts and on certificates of deposit of varying amounts and maturity periods. Since the Ohio and Maryland crises involving state-insured institutions, only institutions with federal insurance are listed.

The yields can be surprisingly high. Here are some examples from September 1986:

| | INTEREST RATE |
|---|---|
| MONEY MARKET ACCOUNTS | |
| Average bank or savings and loan (S&L) | 5.4 percent |
| Meridian Savings, Katy, Texas ([713] 392-1600) | 7.125 percent |
| Colonial National Bank, Wilmington, Delaware ([800] 441-7306) | 7.020 percent |

| | |
|---|---|
| Household Bank, Baltimore, Maryland ([301] 962-5327) | 7.0 percent |

TWO YEAR CERTIFICATES OF DEPOSIT

| | |
|---|---|
| Average bank or S&L | 6.4 percent |
| Sunbelt Savings, Dallas, Texas ([214] 980-4441) | 7.875 percent |
| Charter Savings, Corpus Christi, Texas ([800] 321-1479) | 7.8 percent |
| Pacific Coast S&L, San Francisco, California ([800] 792-7283) | 7.75 percent |

FIVE-YEAR CERTIFICATES OF DEPOSIT

| | |
|---|---|
| Average bank or S&L | 7.2 percent |
| City Savings, Westlake Village, California ([818] 707-0526) | 8.25 percent |
| Nationwide S&L, West Helena, Arkansas ([501] 572-5472) | 8.25 percent |
| Frontier Savings Association, Las Vegas, Nevada ([702] 796-4532) | 8.2 percent |

CDs pay good interest—several percentage points above the inflation rate. So do Treasury bonds, corporate bonds, and mortgage securities. Trouble is, that interest is taxable. Unless your federal income tax bracket is very low, you'll pocket more interest by buying shares in a mutual fund of tax-free "munis"—bonds issued by states or municipalities.

Traditionally, munis have yielded only about half as much as Treasuries or other taxable bonds. But today, the spread has narrowed to three percentage points or less. In fact, some tax-free munis pay higher interest than taxable Treasury bonds. Some investors got the mistaken impression that the new tax law would curtail munis. The law does tighten the rules on certain kinds of municipal bonds, but "general obligation" bonds issued by states and municipalities continue to pay tax-free interest. Municipal bond funds continue to provide excellent tax-free income.

We strongly recommend mutual funds for any kind of bond investment. Most individual bonds cost at least $5,000 each, and the broker pockets a sizable markup. Besides, individual bonds, like individual stocks, require time and expertise. Better to buy into a diversified no-load fund, managed by a professional. It's a simple mail-order purchase that takes no more than a few minutes.

Many investors make the costly mistake of buying bond funds through stockbrokers. Not only are they charged a "load," or sales commission, but they're often steered to bond funds that have performed poorly and that overstate their yield. We cannot emphasize too strongly the importance of avoiding brokers and sticking with straightforward no-load funds such as those listed below.

A bond fund also provides some protection against loss of value. If you buy an individual bond with a face value of $5,000, you'll get interest twice a year, and when the bond matures, you'll get your $5,000 back. But what if you want to sell the bond before it matures? If prevailing interest rates have risen since you bought your bond, you'll get less than $5,000 for it. If interest rates have declined, you'll get more than $5,000. That introduces a speculative factor that few of us want to worry about with a fixed-income investment like a bond.

Bond mutual funds continually buy and sell bonds, so their portfolios include a mix of bonds bought this year, last year, the year before, and so forth. Moreover, the portfolio manager trades with interest-rate fluctuations in mind. So you're partially cushioned against market changes.

For even more secure cushioning, we recommend short-term bond funds. Here's why: The longer a bond's maturity, the more its value will change if interest rates go up or down. Many investors are buying into long-term bond funds, made up of bonds maturing in twenty or thirty years, because the yields are higher. But they're not high enough to warrant the additional risk, in our opinion.

During the inflationary binge of the 1970s, interest rates rose sharply, and long-term bonds lost about half their value. Short-term bonds, maturing in about ten years, lost much less of their value—about 15 percent. We don't expect another climb in interest rates that severe, but no one—absolutely no one—can predict the future course of interest rates. So why not play it safe with short-term bond funds? The yield is about a percentage point less for municipal bond funds, two points for taxable bond funds. That's a sacrifice, but it buys you a lot of safety.

Several mutual fund companies offer an assortment of bond funds. Those with names like "high-income" or "high-yield" are long-term funds and should be avoided. Here are some short-term bond funds that we recommend:

---

TAXABLE BONDS

---

Vanguard Fixed Income Short Term Bond
   Vanguard Financial Center
   P.O. Box 2600
   Valley Forge, Pennsylvania 19482
   ([800] 523-7025)

---

T. Rowe Price New Income Fund
   100 East Pratt Street
   Baltimore, Maryland 21202
   ([800] 638-5660)

---

Fidelity Thrift Trust
   Fidelity Investments
   82 Devonshire Street
   Boston, Massachusetts 02109
   ([800] 544-6666)

---

TAX-EXEMPT BONDS

---

Fidelity Limited—Term Municipals
   Fidelity Investments
   82 Devonshire Street
   Boston, Massachusetts 02109
   ([800] 544-6666)

---

Price Tax-Free Short & Intermediate
   Price Funds, T. Rowe Price Associates
   100 E. Pratt Street
   Baltimore, Maryland 21202
   ([800] 638-1527)

---

Vanguard Municipals Intermediate Term
   Vanguard Financial Center
   Valley Forge, Pennsylvania 19482
   ([800] 523-7025)

---

Before buying, compare yields and average maturities. The shorter the maturity, the safer your investment. *Schabacker's Mutual Fund Quarterly Performance Review*, the newsletter that we recommend, lists and rates both taxable and tax-exempt bond funds.

Brokers and other investment "experts" will tell you that you're foolish to buy anything as plain-vanilla as a CD or a short-term bond fund. They'll sing the praises of investments like Ginnie Maes for income and limited partnerships for tax-sheltered profit. We recommend vanilla. You're investing for yield and safety, not excitement. CDs and bond funds pay off, and while they're paying, you can be pumping iron, playing tennis, or planning the weekend.

## *A Good Tax Shelter That Somehow Survived Tax Reform*

Single-premium whole life insurance is a superb tax-sheltered savings device. It's a worthwhile alternative to municipal bonds, particularly if you're on Social Security.

Don't let the name fool you. Single-premium whole life is a savings device. It's dressed up like life insurance only to take advantage of something very important—a tax exemption that protects life insurance earnings from income tax.

We expected Congress to close this little tax loophole, but it survived the new tax law unscathed.

Let's say that you put $10,000 into the single-premium whole life policy that we recommend—the "Explorer" policy issued by Executive Life of California. As we write this, the yield is 8 percent, guaranteed for five years. Thereafter, the yield will vary in line with prevailing interest rates. Incidentally, that 8 percent yield is about one and one half percentage points above the yield on good municipal bond funds—and it's just as fully sheltered from federal income tax.

Moreover, bonds of any kind fluctuate in value as interest rates rise and fall. You get a bond's face value when it matures, but if you sell it before it matures, you get its market value. A $10,000 single-premium whole life policy is always worth $10,000, plus accumulated earnings.

You can take the yield in cash or let it accumulate and compound, free of income tax. If you are on Social Security, payments from a single-premium whole life policy are preferable to interest on municipal bonds because the federal government now levies what amounts to a light income tax on municipal bond interest received by Social Security pensioners.

You can also withdraw about 85 percent of the principal from your single-premium whole life policy. But never, never drain a single-premium policy of all its cash value and never cancel the policy.

If you do, you'll have to pay income tax on every penny you've ever received from the policy. That's a significant limitation. Single-premium whole life is a good investment if you want tax-free income and don't mind leaving about 15 percent of the principal to your heirs.

Although single-premium whole life is primarily a savings device, you do get some life insurance protection. For $10,000 put into the "Explorer" policy, here's the insurance protection you get:

| IF YOUR AGE IS | YOUR LIFE INSURANCE COVERAGE IS |
| --- | --- |
| 25 | $106,193 |
| 35 | $68,722 |
| 45 | $44,645 |
| 55 | $29,526 |
| 65 | $20,796 |

If you let the interest accumulate and compound, the insurance protection will automatically increase as your policy grows in value.

Single-premium whole life is easy to buy. Call (800) 368-2702 or (301) 762-8150. That's Capitol Financial Services, an insurance broker. Ask for Steve Finkle, executive vice president, and tell him you read about single-premium whole life in this book.

# The Compounding Magic of Reinvestment Plans

With a mutual fund, unlike most stocks, you can choose to have your dividends automatically reinvested in additional shares. You'll be surprised at how quickly your nest egg grows.

Mutual funds offer investors the choice of receiving dividends and capital gains distributions in cash or automatically reinvesting them in additional shares. The compounding arithmetic that results from reinvestment can be sensational.

For example, if you had invested $10,000 in Fidelity Equity Income Fund on October 31, 1975, and had chosen to take your distributions in cash, you would have received checks during the next ten years totaling $21,132. As of October 31, 1985, your shares would have been worth $23,132. So your $10,000 investment would have yielded you $21,132 in cash plus $13,132 in increased value, for a total return of $34,264. Very good.

However, if you had chosen to have all the distributions automatically reinvested, your $10,000 investment would have grown to $92,819, for a return of $82,819. Much better.

The same $10,000 investment in Fidelity Magellan Fund, also on October 31, 1975, would have returned $39,490 in cash distributions during the next ten years. Meantime, the shares would have increased in value to $71,987. Counting cash plus appreciation, the investor would be $101,477 richer—a very nice return.

But if the distributions had been reinvested, that $10,000 investment would have grown in value to $162,909. Quite a difference.

Many investors in individual stocks intend to reinvest their dividends but don't do it consistently. With a dividend check for, say, thirty bucks, it doesn't make sense to call a broker and buy a share of AT&T. That's all you'd get, because the minimum brokerage commission would swallow a big part of your "investment." Anyhow, you can always find a way to spend that thirty bucks.

But a mutual fund will automatically reinvest that dividend in additional shares. You never see the cash, so you don't miss it. Very few mutual funds charge any commission on reinvestments. The process is entirely trouble-free. It's a perfect savings plan for any part-time investor.

When you buy mutual fund shares for an Individual Retirement Account (IRA) or Keogh retirement account, dividends and capital gains distributions will be automatically reinvested. Outside a retirement account, the choice is yours. If you want the money to spend, take your distributions in cash. If you want to build up a nest egg, have your distributions automatically reinvested.

# What to Do with a Windfall

Inheritances of $100,000 or more have become common. What would you do with an unexpected windfall?

If you believe in our philosophy, you already know that financial planning doesn't have to be a drag. *Financial planning* is a pretentious term that simply means this: in picking the right financial tools, we all have to consider our unique personal situations. There's no better or more pleasant way to illustrate these differences than to drop a fat make-believe windfall on people of different ages and circumstances and help them invest it—or spend it.

In fact, windfalls aren't a bit rare. Few of us will win a lottery or break the bank at Atlantic City or Las Vegas. But inheritances of $100,000 or more occur frequently, even among people of modest circumstances, largely because real estate values have multiplied during the past decade or so and stock prices have risen sharply over the past four years.

If your parents leave you their three-bedroom house, your windfall will almost surely be worth at least $100,000. It could be worth several times that much. The federal estate tax no longer touches estates of $600,000 or less. Moreover, you can sell inherited property immediately without paying federal income tax. (If it increases in value after you inherit it, you pay tax on the difference between the value at the time of inheritance and the selling price.) So you can turn inherited real estate or securities into cash, and that cash is all yours—a true windfall.

Now, how do you invest that money for the greatest benefit to you and your family? That depends largely on your age, circumstances, attitudes, and goals. Let's drop $100,000 on three individuals or couples and help them invest it wisely. Chances are you'll find yourself somewhere in these portraits. In every case, a financial planner could come up with investment plans that would require lots of time and trouble. We'll stick with our basic approach.

Our first windfall recipient is Roberta French, age thirty, who makes $30,000 a year. Roberta is single. She owes $80,000 on her townhouse and $3,000 on credit card balances. Her company has no pension plan. Roberta contributes $2,000 a year to her Individual Retirement Account (IRA), which is now worth $5,000. She has little cash.

Roberta should start with the dead-dry conservative stuff. She should pay her credit card bills first. Then she should take out a disability insurance policy (see Lesson 41) to support herself in case she becomes unable to work. Next, she ought to set up a power of attorney, naming a brother or sister or close friend to manage her affairs in case she, for some unforeseen reason, cannot.

Planning for her old age, Roberta should continue her IRA contributions, not expecting the IRA to provide all the money she'll need in retirement. Because her company has no pension plan, she is entitled to deduct the full $2,000 IRA contribution every year, just as she did before enactment of the new tax law. She should put $10,000 of her windfall into a single-premium whole life insurance policy and leave it there. The interest will compound free of income tax, just like an IRA. Assuming the yield averages 8 percent, her $10,000 policy will be worth $100,627 in thirty years. In retirement, or during any period of need, she can withdraw money, free of federal income tax. See Lesson 28 for details.

Now for some fun. Roberta might like a beach cottage or a ski condo, and if so, she should buy one, rent it out, or use it herself (see Lesson 34). She'll have to shop carefully to make sure she's buying at a good price and picking a property that will appeal to vacation tenants as well as to her. A rental property provides tax write-offs and should increase in value.

Even though mortgage interest continues to be deductible, we are not fans of big mortgages. To get the deduction, she has to pay the interest, and every penny spent on interest is a penny she can't spend on more pleasant alternatives. Let's assume she buys a vacation property for $100,000. We'd suggest that she put $40,000 down and take a variable-rate mortgage covering the remaining $60,000.

Roberta still has about $55,000 of her windfall. She should put $30,000 in mutual funds that are likely to produce nice growth, choosing two from the list in Lesson 21 and investing $15,000 in each, with dividends automatically reinvested so her nest egg will grow. She should put $20,000 into a mutual fund that holds tax-exempt municipal bonds, picking one from those we recommended in Lesson 27, and have the interest paid to her so she can handle her mortgage payments without feeling pinched.

That leaves five thousand bucks for Roberta to enjoy.


Our next lucky people are Ralph and Jane Seaman. They're in their late thirties and have three children, all of whom will be starting college within the next five to ten years. The children are good students, and the Seamans want them to attend the best colleges they can, no matter the cost.

Ralph and Jane have secure jobs. Between them, they make $60,000 a year. They live comfortably but have little money saved and owe $50,000 on their mortgage. The Seamans should devote a large portion of their $100,000 windfall to their children's education, in a way that will save on taxes. We cover paying for college thoroughly in Lesson 38; here's an abbreviated version tailored for the Seamans.

Ralph and Jane can give each child as much as $20,000 a year without paying federal gift tax. The new tax law limits the benefits of giving money to children, but leaves a good deal of elbow room. For a child under 14 years old, the first $1,000 a year in interest or dividends on investments that were a gift is taxed at the child's tax bracket, which is usually low or nil. Interest or dividends above $1,000 a year are taxed at the parents' highest tax bracket, which is usually much higher than the child's. For a child 14 or older, all income, without limit, is taxed at the child's tax brackets.

The Seamans could immediately give each child about $11,000 and invest that money for them in high-yield CDs that will mature just when the cash is needed for tuition. (See Lesson 27 for how to find the highest-yielding CDs.) At current CD interest rates, $11,000 will yield just under the $1,000 a year limit. At the same time, Ralph and Jane could each buy a $10,000 single-premium whole life policy and let the tax-free earnings accumulate (see Lesson 28). As each child reaches 14, the Seamans could check whether they would net more, after taxes, by keeping the money in the single-premium policy until college bills come due or by withdrawing some of it and using the proceeds to buy a CD in the child's name.

Here's an alternative that is a little riskier but offers prospects for a greater payoff. The Seamans could give, say, $15,000 to each child, investing $7,500 in a CD and the other $7,500 in one of the growth mutual funds that we recommend in Lesson 21. The CD will yield between $600 and $700 a year in interest, safely below the $1,000 limit. The mutual fund will yield little in dividends, but is likely to gain substantially in value. That gain will not be not taxed until it is cashed in—in other words, until the mutual fund shares are sold. The Seaman children won't cash it in until they're ready for college. By then they will be older than 14, so their profit on the mutual fund shares will be taxed to them in their bracket rather than their parents' higher bracket.

By putting money toward their children's education, the Seamans are benefiting themselves, too, because they otherwise would be borrowing and using part of their income for college tuition. Assuming the Seamans can count on generous retirement pensions, they can use the remainder of their windfall for investments of their choice. They, too, might like to buy a vacation home and rent it out. They might want to invest in a mutual fund (Lesson 21), a municipal bond fund for tax-free income (Lesson 27), or a real estate investment trust for income and capital gain (Lesson 33). And they might like to reserve $5,000 or $10,000 for travel or other pleasurable pursuits.

Joe and Ann Cavanagh are in their fifties, have no children, and together make $100,000 a year. So why do people like the Cavanaghs need a windfall?

Because Joe and Ann outspend their income. They owe $100,000 on their mortgage, and their credit card debts amount to $10,000. Their retirement accounts total $40,000. That's not much for people of their age and circumstances.

The Cavanaghs have been paying about half of their income in taxes. The new tax law helps them, because it reduces their federal income tax bracket from 42 percent in 1986 to 35 percent in 1987 and to 28 percent starting in 1988. They should quickly pay off their credit card debts, the more so since interest on that kind of consumer debt is no longer fully deductible.

They should then look into a tax-sheltered real estate investment. For the Cavanaghs, a year-round rental property might work better than a vacation home; they could buy a house or a small office building.

For big spenders like Joe and Ann, a real estate investment has the virtue of tying up their money while saving on taxes and building equity. For the same reasons, we'd urge them to put $20,000 each in single-premium whole life insurance policies (see Lesson 28). These policies are designed to produce tax-sheltered savings, and if the Cavanaghs let the earnings accumulate, they'll build substantial nest eggs from which they can withdraw in retirement, free of federal income tax. As an incidental benefit, the policies will provide the Cavanaghs with life insurance. He can be the beneficiary of her policy, she of his.

They should invest $10,000 in each of two capital gains mutual funds from the list in Lesson 21 and have the dividends reinvested. With the remaining $10,000, they should go to town—or to Tahiti or Bali or Paris or an antique store or anyplace else that grabs their fancy.

Our beneficiaries vary a great deal in age and circumstances. Yet each can meet personal goals with the help of investments that fit our reliable and profitable time-saving approach—equity mutual funds, municipal bond funds, real estate, single-premium whole life insurance. These are workhorse investments that can pull the load whatever your age and situation.

# LESSON 31

## *Avoiding Fees and Commissions*

Try to hold down commissions and other investment fees. Extra fees contribute nothing to the quality of your investment.

Every mutual fund charges an annual management fee, typically about 1 percent of the fund's assets. That's quite reasonable, assuming the fund is performing well. One percent of, say, $100 million is a million bucks. That's plenty to pay the rent and handsomely compensate the fund manager and the other employees.

Trouble is, many funds charge other fees, too. Those additional fees serve three purposes, none of which benefits you: They add to the company's profits. They fatten the paychecks of managers or brokers. And they enable the company to spend more on advertising.

Competition in the investment business has prompted many firms to hide their charges. Instead of charging you a commission, or "load," up front, they deduct an annual management fee that is larger than normal or charge the fund for marketing expenses or charge you a redemption fee when you cash in your shares.

In comparing mutual funds or any other kind of investment, take all these charges into account. To find them, you'll have to read the fund's prospectus—the booklet that any fund will send you when you call to inquire about investing. A fund that charges higher fees has to make up that extra ground to stay even with a pure no-load fund.

Performance is still the foremost consideration. For example, Fidelity Magellan charges a "load" of 3 percent, but we continue to recommend it because it has outperformed all other mutual funds during the past decade.

But never let a sales rep persuade you that a higher fee gives you better management. From your standpoint, fees and commissions are negative factors. Weigh them accordingly.

# Swindles—One Growth Industry You Should Avoid

Investment swindles have become an epidemic, and their victims include sophisticated lawyers and businesspeople who should know better. Don't assume that you're too smart to get conned. Stick to straightforward and conventional investments that you thoroughly understand and don't let greed get the best of your judgment.

Jack Anderson has won fame and a Pulitzer Prize for his investigative reporting, an occupation that requires a suspicious attitude toward people in high places. But Anderson wasn't suspicious enough when it came to one of his investments; he bought into a pyramid scheme.

Economist Arthur Laffer, creator of the "Laffer curve," got curved himself in a tax-shelter scam. So did Peter F. Krogh, dean of the School of Foreign Service at Georgetown University. Other victims of securities and tax-shelter scams have included partners in prominent law and accounting firms, New York superlawyer Victor Kovner, entertainers Woody Allen and Dick Cavett, and author Erica Jong.

In mid-1985, the North American Securities Administrators Association (1400 I St. N.W., Washington, D.C. 20005) reported on a nationwide survey of fraudulent get-rich-quick schemes, with this conclusion: "The current era of confusion and chaos is a made-to-order incubator for financial fraud, which has emerged as nothing short of a boom industry today." *Forbes* magazine says more people are being fleeced today than in 1929.

You could be next. Today's con artists deal in investments that sound very good. They prey on everyone's desire to make more money and pay less tax. They use the status of prestigious addresses and famous friends. They win trust by employing "affinity group" salesmanship—Mormons selling to Mormons, fraternity grads to fellow brothers, businesswomen to business-women, even gays to gays.

The numbers of victims, and the famous names, are just the tip of the iceberg. Most con victims are too embarrassed to admit it.

The public's gullibility results from three things. One is today's freewheeling investment market, which seems to turn out a new product every day. Most new investment products are created simply to give salespeople something to talk about. When someone calls you up to describe a new investment or tax shelter, hang up, unless you're willing to spend the hours and hours it would take to thoroughly investigate the offering.

Second is the inflation hangover from the 1970s, when people saw their savings lose ground to rising prices while their incomes, although gaining little or nothing in purchasing power, pushed them into higher tax brackets. Many people became desperate and couldn't resist get-rich-quick schemes.

Third and most important is the narcotic effect of greed. When someone tells you that an investment can earn 25 percent a year, you *want* to believe it. Sweetened with today's sophisticated sales pitches, these scams are hard to resist. From the pitch and the prospectus, you can't tell whether the offering is legal or fraudulent, safe or unsafe. You simply have to say no to any investment that you do not thoroughly understand.

Remember, you can safely earn 6 percent or more, free of income tax (see Lesson 27). That's way above today's inflation rate. You can legally and profitably reduce your income tax by employing other strategies in this book. You can invest in sound, proven mutual funds with a historical record of earning 15 percent or more a year. None of these proven strategies takes much time or requires you to talk to a salesperson, and none of them will add your name to the growing list of fraud victims.

# *Trouble-Free Real Estate Investing*

Real estate investment trusts got a black eye a decade ago, but they have come back strongly. The new tax law enhances their appeal. If you want to put money in real estate without worrying about tenants, plumbers, and other such concerns, invest in a blue-chip REIT and enjoy the dividends.

In 1960, Congress decided it would be nice to attract the money of ordinary investors into office buildings, shopping centers, apartment complexes, and other commercial real estate developments. So our lawmakers created a unique tax-favored investment called the real estate investment trust, or REIT (pronounced "reet").

A REIT pays no federal tax. To qualify for that tax exemption—in other words, to make itself into a REIT—a developer has to invest at least 75 percent of its assets in real estate and has to distribute at least 95 percent of its income to shareholders. Moreover, a REIT has to make its living developing property and renting it out, not buying and selling. To keep out speculators, the law says that a REIT has to hold a piece of property for at least four years. A REIT can't sell more than five properties in a year, no matter how many properties it owns. In exchange for meeting these restrictions, the REIT operator gets something very valuable in return: a 100 percent exemption from federal tax.

That sounds like the kind of investment that might have been curbed by the new tax law, but it was not. In fact, the new tax law streamlined the benefits of REITs even more. And since the new tax law makes dividends more attractive by lowering income tax rates, REITs, with their high dividends, benefit more than most other investments. One Wall Street analyst called the new tax law a "REIT relief act."

So there you are: a neatly packaged real estate investment—ideal if you consider commercial real estate a growth business. Investing in a REIT is akin to investing in one of the specialized "sector" mutual funds that are devoted to a single industry, such as health care or technology.

A REIT works much like a mutual fund, except that you have to buy REIT shares through a stockbroker. Nowhere else in this book do we recommend that you contact a stockbroker, but if you're interested in REITs, you have no choice.

We recommend two brokerage firms. Both are "discount" brokers; their commissions are low, and they do not bother you with advice. You call them when you want to buy or sell. Otherwise, they leave you alone. You'll first have to set up an account. To get forms and information, call one of the toll-free numbers. The firms:

| | |
|---|---|
| PACIFIC BROKERAGE SERVICES | (800) 421-8395 nationwide |
| | (800) 421-3214 in California |
| | (800) 221-5281 in Florida |
| | (800) 522-5005 in New York |
| | (800) 621-6593 in Illinois |
| | (800) 442-5603 in Texas |
| DISCOUNT BROKERAGE CORPORATION | (800) 221-5088 nationwide |
| | (212) 806-2700 in New York State |

Because they pay no federal tax and have to distribute 95 percent of their income to shareholders, REITs pay healthy dividends—typically two or three or four percentage points more than a regular corporation or mutual fund. In fact, many corporations and some mutual funds pay very little in dividends or none at all. They're not required to pay dividends; a REIT is, assuming it earns a profit.

You pay income tax on REIT dividends; it is the REIT, not its shareholders, that is sheltered from income tax. Of course, most corporations pay corporate income tax on their profits, and their shareholders pay income tax on dividends—the "double taxation of dividends" that some people would like to abolish. It's already been abolished for REITs. As a result, REITs have more income to distribute to their shareholders.

You can choose from four kinds of REITs. An "equity REIT" is ideal if you are seeking income plus an eventual capital gain in the value of the stock. An equity REIT builds (or buys) commercial real estate, rents it out, and tries to boost its value, and its rent, by upgrading the property. For example, a REIT might buy a neighborhood shopping center, expand and improve it, attract glitzier stores serving a wealthier clientele, and triple the rents. That's not farfetched; it happens all the time.

A "mortgage REIT" lends money to builders and developers. It's an income investment, very much like buying a mutual fund that deals in mortgage securities or a bond fund (see Lesson 27). An "equity-mortgage combination REIT" does some of both. A "participating mortgage REIT" makes loans and ties each loan to some kind of participation in the deal, in hopes of getting some growth in addition to mortgage interest.

According to *Audit's Realty Stock Review,* a very good investors' newsletter, yields in August 1986 averaged 7.5 percent for equity REITs, 10.7 percent for mortgage REITs, 8.7 percent for property-mortgage combination REITs, and 9.5 percent for participating mortgage REITs. (If you're interested in subscribing to the newsletter, call [201] 358-2735 or write to Audit's Realty Stock Review, 136 Summit Avenue, Suite 200, Montvale, New Jersey 07645.)

Your choice of a REIT depends on your goals. We asked Kenneth D. Campbell, president of *Audit's Realty Stock Review,* to recommend REITs in each category. Campbell emphasizes that his choices are based on the quality of the company but are not up-to-date "buy" recommendations, because a "buy" is based partly on the current price of the stock, and he has no way of knowing how the price will stand when you read this. Remember, you can only buy REITs from a stockbroker (see our recommendation of brokerage houses earlier in the lesson), so we've omitted telephone numbers below.

EQUITY REITs

Federal Realty
    5454 Wisconsin Avenue, Suite 1100
    Chevy Chase, Maryland 20815

First Union Real Estate
    55 Public Square, Suite 1900
    Cleveland, Ohio 44113

HRE Properties
    530 Fifth Avenue
    New York, New York 10036

MORTGAGE REITs

MONY Mortgage Investments
    1740 Broadway, Mail Drop 17-23
    New York, New York 10019

Mortgage and Realty Trust
    9200 Sunset Boulevard, P.O. Box 69370
    Los Angeles, California 90069

| EQUITY-MORTGAGE COMBINATION REIT |
| --- |
| Property Capital Trust<br>   200 Clarendon Street<br>   Hancock Tower, 47th Floor<br>   Boston, Massachusetts 02116 |
| PARTICIPATING MORTGAGE REITs |
| L&N Housing Corp.<br>   2001 Bryan Tower, Suite 3600<br>   Dallas, Texas 75201 |
| Mellon Participating Mortgage<br>   551 Madison Avenue<br>   New York, New York 10022 |

REITs got a bad name in the 1970s. They attracted more investment money than they could intelligently digest, and some REIT managers borrowed and built unwisely. Today, REITs tend to be managed more prudently. But don't buy just any REIT, any more than you would buy just any mutual fund. Pick a winner with goals in line with yours.

# Tax-Sheltered Real Estate
# Close to Home

Investing in real estate close to home can be one of the easiest, safest, and most profitable ways for your money to grow. Real estate investments have historically made money, lots of money, for investors. And probably the technique that makes the most sense is to purchase rental real estate in your neighborhood or town.

Quick now: Which of these deals would you be most comfortable with?

1. A limited partnership, described in a two-hundred-page prospectus that tells you about a shopping center project located hundreds of miles from your home. To participate in it, you have to commit several thousand dollars a year for three or four years. You have to entrust your money to a stranger. You must be confident that the IRS will go along with the glowing tax opinion offered in the prospectus. And while the prospectus may not say so (or if it does, it's in very bland terms), as much as 30 percent of your investment may be soaked up by commissions and fees that line the sales rep's pockets. If you decide to get out of the partnership prior to the date it matures, chances are you'll suffer a steep loss, even if the property has increased in value, because there is a very small market for your interest. It's tough to sell. And any losses you have will not be deductible, but rather will have to be offset against tax shelter profits, if you have any!
2. A house, townhouse, or condominium located near yours that you can buy and rent out. You pay closing costs when you purchase the real estate. You can sell anytime you want. Any losses you have will probably be tax deductible.

Which do you understand better—a limited partnership or rental real estate? Which do you consider most likely to appreciate in value in the short term and over the long haul? If you rely on the advice of an investment broker, don't be surprised if he recommends the limited partnership. That, after all, is how he makes a living—collecting commissions off of the sales he makes.

If you make your investment decisions yourself, and we hope that you do, then you should probably choose the nearby house or condominium. Here's why. You almost certainly know your own city and neighborhood much better than you do some distant locale. You know which neighborhoods are trendy, which are rebuilding, and which are going downhill. Investing in rental real estate close to home means that you know what you're buying, as opposed to purchasing distant property through a stranger. For those reasons, real estate that you purchase and rent out close to home is for many Americans the most familiar and savvy of investment choices, especially now that the 1986 Tax Reform Act has closed down so many other tax sheltered investments.

Real estate is not a get-rich-quick scheme, although it has been known to happen from time to time and place to place. In the inflationary real estate boom of the 1970s, investors were known to buy properties for $100,000 one month and turn around and sell them for $150,000 the next. However, those situations are few and far between.

Traditionally, you should look at real estate as a long-term investment. Unlike shares of stock you purchase in a mutual fund or corporation, or a bond you buy from the U.S. Treasury Department, a house is neither bought nor sold overnight. The process frequently takes months. In addition, there are closing fees, title searches, attorney charges, and recording taxes that eat into your profits. All these argue for you to hold the property as it appreciates and as you enjoy your tax benefits.

In fact, we recommend that you hold on to real estate investments for a minimum of five years. If you want to get a good deal on the right house at the right price in the right neighborhood, you can't be in a hurry. For the same reason, you can't be in a hurry to sell.

During the past decade, housing prices have increased more than twice as rapidly as salaries. That's impressive. Many smart investors poured their money into items of solid value during the late 1970s when inflation was roaring along at double-digit rates. High on that list was real estate. Those who bought real estate then did very well indeed.

But today, inflation is hovering right between 2 and 4 percent and has remained there for the past three years. Housing prices have generally leveled off. In fact, in some parts of the country, the price of homes has dropped. You cannot count on inflationary increases to boost the value of real estate. However, over a period of years, well-chosen real estate has historically returned excellent profits. And that's a trend we don't expect to change.

OK. You're ready to go out and look for that house or townhouse to buy so you can join the ranks of the landlords. But when you do, you may find that it will cost you more cash each month to service the mortgage than you will collect in rent. You will experience what's called a negative cash flow. It will take a couple of years of regular rent increases for you to break even.

So what's the benefit of losing money every month? There are two—one long-term and the other short. The long-term benefit is that the well-chosen property should increase in value over the years. You pay no tax on that increase until such time as you decide to sell.

And in the short term, you can enjoy the tax benefits associated with real estate ownership. Certainly, the tax code sweetens the pot considerably by granting deductions for real estate taxes paid, interest on mortgage loans, maintenance, and other rental expenses, plus depreciation.

Here's what the new tax law has to say about residential real estate investments.

As a general rule, all tax sheltered investments, real estate included, are considered to be "passive" in nature. And losses from these passive investments (purchased after the new law was enacted) may not be deductible against your salary, wages, dividends, interest and business profits, but rather have to be offset against profits from similar passive investments. If you don't have sufficient passive profits, then you will have to carry over your unusued losses to a future year when you do. Either that, or claim your loss in the year you sell your investment. Stock market investors take note: Securities transactions are considered "active" and profits from them cannot be used to offset passive losses, or vice versa.

So, what's the point of investing in residential real estate when you may not be able to deduct your losses? In fact, there is a gaping exception to the rule above. All you have to do is take an active role in your properties and have income under $100,000.

You cannot just turn over your interest in a townhouse to a management firm. You have to help select the tenant, hire the plumber to fix the leak (or do it yourself), paint the rooms, and so on. By actively managing your property, you bring yourself to the next obstacle. If your annual income is below $100,000 a year, you can deduct against your salary, wages and other regular income up to $25,000 of your net losses from the operation of your rental activity. Excess losses get the same tax shelter treatment described earlier. If your income is above $150,000, you get none of the deduction. Congress feels you're too rich and don't need the tax break. If your income falls between $100,000 and $150,000 you get a ratable deduction.

That brings us to depreciation, one of the kindest tax breaks of all, or at least it used to be.

In 1981, Congress decided to cut taxes across the board. Specifically, in an effort to revive an ailing housing industry, Congress voted almost unbelievably generous tax breaks to landlords in the form of accelerated depreciation deductions for property placed in service after 1980. The giveaway has been modified since then.

In addition to voting accelerated depreciation, Congress made the depreciation deductions so straightforward that the IRS couldn't question them. Earlier, real estate investors could almost count on being audited by the IRS. When an investor said a piece of rental property would wear out over twenty-five years, the IRS would say it would take thirty-five or forty years. If you said forty, the IRS would say fifty. There was always an argument, and for the most part, the IRS would win because you couldn't prove the IRS was incorrect.

Under the newest depreciation system, the tax law specifies the number of years over which you can depreciate your property. Currently, it's 27.5 years for newly purchased residential real estate, and 31.5 years for commercial real estate. With both classifications, depreciation is taken on a straight-line basis—that is, the same amount each year.

Studies indicate that the best kind of house, townhouse, or condominium to purchase for rental is one that is moderately priced. You don't want to buy the most expensive place or the cheapest. Find the middle ground and invest there. You might buy a house in a nice area of your town for, say, $75,000. Of that, roughly $25,000 would be for the land, with the remaining $50,000 for the house. That distinction is important for tax reasons. You can only depreciate the building, not the land. Even the IRS knows that land doesn't wear out. Your local tax appraiser makes the breakdown between the house and the property for you; just refer to the real estate assessment.

Once you buy a place, you expect it to go up in value. You wouldn't knowingly buy one that would become less valuable over the years. Yet, happily, that is precisely what the tax law says is going to happen. The house is going to wear out. That wearing out is called depreciation. Depreciation is nothing more than a subtraction from your income—in this case, a subtraction from your rental income. If you have more depreciation than rental income, you can use the excess according to the new rules mentioned earlier.

A cautionary note is in order here. Depreciation deductions only come into play for rental and other investment property. They are not available to those who use a property as a personal residence.

Keep in mind that the depreciation rules can change. Congress is notorious for that. We mentioned earlier that property owned prior to 1981 was depreciated over a period of time that the tax-payer and the IRS negotiated. Since then, the depreciation periods have been precisely specified:

- For property placed in service between 1981 and March 15, 1984, the depreciation period was fifteen years.
- For property placed in service between March 16, 1984, and May 8, 1985, the depreciation period was eighteen years.
- Property placed in service after May 8, 1985, and before 1987, can be depreciated over nineteen years.

At this point, you can be confident that unless Congress changes the law between the time we are writing this book and the time it is published, you can claim straight line depreciation over 27.5 years, deducting 3.64 percent of its cost per year.

In addition to the depreciation deduction, you also get to deduct out-of-pocket expenses associated with the property. They include the interest portion of your mortgage payment, real estate taxes, and maintenance costs. Each of these tax-saving deductions is worth money to you.

Ideally, you want your rental income and tax savings to produce a positive, or at least a break-even, cash flow. However, during the first few years you own the property, it's unlikely that rental income will reach the level of your mortgage expense and upkeep. Nonetheless, your tax benefits should go a long way to closing the gap.

Don't be dazzled merely by the tax savings built into real estate investment. They're valuable, and you can use them to justify a purchase of property. But the key is to choose the right property at the right price, negotiate the right mortgage, and manage your new asset wisely. And that's a much easier task when you invest close to home rather than with a stranger who is pouring your money into a limited partnership thousands of miles away.

# JUNE

## *Your Home*

Your home is an ideal investment because it is an essential shelter, a valuable asset, and a superb tax saver. If you work at home, the tax benefits are even greater. Shop as carefully for a mortgage as you shop for your home; the right mortgage could save you thousands of dollars.

 *To Do*

- Monthly budget
- Second estimated tax payment due June 15
- Tax return due by June 15 if you were out of the country on April 15
- Invest to maximize dollar-cost averaging (see page 100)
- Second tax review session of the year at the end of June (see page 45)
- If you have a 30-year mortgage, figure the extra monthly expense of turning it into a 15-year mortgage; if you can afford it, do it

- What business can you operate on the side out of your home? (See page 156)

# *You Don't Own Your Home?*
# *You Should*

Owning your home can provide you with more financial security than any other single investment. A well-chosen home can increase in value over the years, throw off huge tax benefits, boost the value of other tax deductions, furnish you with a place to start your own business, generate a tax-free retirement nest egg, and provide a major portion of your estate.

It's the American dream to own a home or at least to have one that's subject to a mortgage. If you don't presently own a home, chances are you either did at one time (before you retired) or are planning to purchase one in the future.

In the 1970s, the price of housing increased at a tremendous rate. Homes that originally sold for $30,000 skyrocketed to three and four times that. You couldn't lose. People would buy the most expensive house they could afford, struggle with the mortgage payments for a few years, sell at a big profit, and buy another, still more expensive home. And they would repeat the process two and three times.

The inflationary spiral has subsided. Real estate is no longer guaranteed to increase so rapidly in value. In fact, in some parts of the country, housing has actually dropped in value. Yet over the long term, housing continues to be a terrific investment, one that is difficult to pass up.

Over the past year or so, a handful of financial professionals have recommended against buying a home. We disagree. They calculate that, under certain circumstances, you can come out ahead by renting rather than buying, and you should certainly run through the numbers, figuring out how best to invest your money. But we feel that a well-selected home can prove to be one of the better investments around, especially at this time of more reasonable interest rates. We are both homeowners and recommend to others that they own, too. Our homes are worth much more than we paid for them, and our mortgage payments are less than what we would be paying to rent comparable housing.

Here are seven financial incentives to home ownership:

First, the property will appreciate in value over the years. Of course, there are no promises, but the statistics are strongly in your favor. The value of a well-chosen piece of real estate will probably keep pace with or even exceed inflation. What's more, you don't have to pay tax on this appreciation until you sell—and maybe not even then.

When you sell your personal residence, you have to report the deal to the IRS on Form 2119, "Sale or Exchange of Personal Residence," when you file your return for that year. But chances are you won't have to fork over a dime in income tax. The law has a special out for you. It says you aren't taxed on your housing profits if you purchase a more expensive personal residence within two years of the sale. Because the price of housing keeps going up, most people do end up purchasing a more expensive home within the two-year period. If you don't replace the property within this time limit, your profit will be taxed. In the unlikely event you suffer a loss, it is not deductible under the tax law.

It is not the least bit unusual to find people today living in homes valued at $150,000 (and up) who originally paid $50,000 for them years ago. The same possibility of long-term appreciation exists today for the home buyer.

Second, the tax benefits of home ownership are almost too good to be true. When you purchase a place, you can deduct a large portion of the settlement costs. You can also deduct the interest you pay on your home mortgage as well as the real estate taxes you pay to your local government. While a renter is often saddled with the short tax form, a homeowner files the long form to take advantage of every possible deduction. The IRS rarely asks for verification because housing deductions are so straightforward.

The only deduction you don't get is one for depreciation. That only comes into play when you use a portion of your home for business pursuits or decide to hold on to the house and turn it into rental property when you move.

Congress scaled back or entirely eliminated many tax breaks that people have been used to. But two that were untouched are the deductions for mortgage interest and real estate taxes. In fact, you can deduct these on a second or vacation home as well.

Third, the value of your other tax deductions is greatly enhanced. Many taxpayers who are not homeowners can't itemize their deductions on Schedule A. They enjoy no tax benefit for their medical expenses, other interest payments, miscellaneous deductions, and the like. The reason is these deductions do not reach the level of the standard deduction. For example, in 1986, the standard deduction for a married couple filing jointly was $3,670. For single taxpayers, it was $2,480. (The amounts increase annually to reflect inflation.) If you didn't own your home, chances are you didn't have enough itemized deductions to list on Schedule A.

But if you did own your home and paid mortgage interest and real estate taxes, you would have easily exceeded these levels. And as a result, you also took further advantage of the many other tax deductions available to you.

Fourth, your home can be the source of all your future borrowing. Because of the 1986 Tax Reform Act, your tax deduction for consumer interest (that's what you pay on credit card balances, auto and student loans, and other installment debt) is restricted. While it was 100 percent deductible in 1986, only 65 percent can be written off in 1987, 40 percent in 1988, 20 percent in 1989, and 10 percent in 1990. After 1990, no consumer or personal interest will be deductible.

But interest you pay on your home mortgage and a second or vacation property is. So, when you need money to pay for a car or vacation, school or medical bills, to add on to the house, or for any other worthwhile purpose, you should consider either refinancing your mortgage or taking out a second. Either way, you are tapping into your home equity to pay for an expense that you would otherwise finance with loans on which you could not fully deduct the interest. You are trading one interest expense for another, the only difference being that when you borrow against your house, the interest is deductible, and when you borrow on credit cards and from GMAC, the interest is not deductible.

An important point to keep in mind when tapping your home equity with a line of credit is that you must repay the loan. Certainly, it is your home equity, but it is still the bank's money. They want it back with interest.

There is an exception to this borrowing opportunity. Congress ruled that you can borrow no more than the original price of the house plus the cost of improvements that you put into it over the years.

Say, for example, that your home cost you $40,000 some years ago, and you have put another $20,000 into it to build a deck, pave the drive, and add a family room. Your cost basis is $60,000, while you might owe only $15,000 on the original mortgage note. If today the property's fair market value is $115,000, you can borrow up to $77,000. (That's 80 percent of today's value less the outstanding mortgage loan balance.)

Borrow that much and you could find yourself with a tax problem. You will have exceeded your tax basis in the property by $17,000.

But as a practical matter, few people will want or need to borrow such large amounts. Even a fancy new car only costs $20,000.

In addition, there's an exception to the exception. While the general rule is you can borrow no more than your cost in the property, you can borrow more when the money is used to pay for medical bills, education expenses, and more home improvements.

Fifth, entrepreneurs need a location where they can get started, and it should be cheap. Budding businesses have a hard time affording expensive rents. There's no place better suited than your home. There may be zoning restrictions against operating a home business in your residential neighborhood, but a one-person operation can frequently be exempted. And there are a whole raft of tax breaks available to you when you operate a business out of your home. See Lesson 37 for more details.

Sixth, you can lay the foundation of your retirement around your home. Take this situation: You buy your first home in your twenties or early thirties. You sell and buy, typically, three or four times during your work career. Each time, you purchase a larger, more costly home. Taxes on the profits have been deferred because you kept buying progressively more expensive homes. Now it's time for retirement. The children are grown, and you no longer need as large a house as you've had in the past.

A wonderful tax break known as the "age fifty-five rule" now comes to your aid to prevent the taxation of the profit you make when you sell the property. Here's how it works.

When you sell your personal residence after you celebrate your fifty-fifth birthday, you can pocket as much as $125,000 of your profit, tax-free. There are a few other restrictions, but they aren't tough to sidestep. You must have lived in the house a minimum of three out of the past five years. If you're married, you have to file a joint return with both husband and wife agreeing to this $125,000 profit exclusion. It's good only one time; once you've used it, you can never use it again. If your profit is under $125,000 and you make this tax election, you lose any unused portion. For example, if your profit is $100,000 and you take the election, you lose out on the other $25,000 available to you.

Say you purchased a home years ago for $25,000. You sell for $150,000 and plan to retire. You can take that full $125,000 without any reduction for income taxes and invest it at, say, 10 percent, generating $12,500 a year in retirement income. Not bad.

After you sell, and pocket your profit tax-free, you still need a place to live. You can go out and purchase a smaller place that will suit your needs and still enjoy the real estate tax and mortgage interest deductions. Or you can combine the regular tax deferral (when you sell one property and purchase a more expensive residence) with the $125,000 exclusion. This comes into play most frequently when someone sells a home for a profit of more than $125,000 and purchases, say, a condominium for much less than the sale price of the old house. Say the profit is $150,000. Of this amount, $125,000 can be excluded automatically. The tax on the remaining $25,000 is deferred because the new condo costs more than that amount. It's not a difficult computation. It's all explained on Form 2119.

The seventh and final incentive to home ownership is that the value of your personal residence can make up the major portion of your estate. It's not unusual these days for a personal residence and its surrounding property to run into hundreds of thousands of dollars. When you prepare your net worth statement (see Lesson 7), you're asked to note in the assets column the fair market value of your home and to list the remaining amount of your mortgage in the liabilities column. The difference is what someone would get for your property by selling it. Compare that amount with your net worth. Chances are your house makes up a substantial portion of your estate.

When your time comes, much of the money your heirs inherit will likely come from the sale of the house or from the cash you invested from its earlier sale.

There are many pluses to owning a home. If you don't already, you should. You're missing out on too many financial benefits. If you already do, you've made a good choice. Now make certain that you enjoy all the tax benefits that are available to you, especially when you start an at-home business or plan for your retirement.

# LESSON 36

## *Saving $100,000 or More with the Best Mortgage*

Saving on your mortgage is easy. We're not talking about nickels and dimes here. You can voluntarily pay over to the mortgage company $100,000 or more in extra interest it doesn't deserve, or you can spend the cash on yourself. It's your choice.

Most Americans consider their personal residences to be their biggest investments, but they aren't. It's not the house that's so expensive; it's the mortgage loan you take out to finance the house.

Let's say you buy a home for $125,000, paying $25,000 down and financing the remaining $100,000 with a fixed-rate, thirty-year mortgage. The interest rate is 10 percent. You'll pay $877.58 a month to cover your loan-repayment obligation. Over thirty years, that amounts to $315,928.80, of which $215,928.80 is interest. Fortunately, there is more than one technique you can use to reduce the high price of home ownership.

Paying interest, even mortgage interest, is not all it's cracked up to be. (Read Lesson 47, where we go into detail about the false promise of interest deductions.) It all boils down to this—you have to earn the money to pay the interest charges. True, you enjoy an income tax deduction for what you pay in interest. But that can be terribly misleading. Take a look at the numbers. Say you're in the 28 percent income tax bracket and remain there throughout the period of time you own the house. Assuming the same example, the $215,929 you pay in interest will result in a tax benefit of $60,460 over the years. You, on the other hand, will have had to dig into your pocket to come up with the remaining $155,469. No matter how you view it, that's still a lot of money.

Here are three alternatives to paying so much interest to your lender.

First, you can turn your thirty-year, fixed-rate mortgage into a fifteen-year loan. There are plenty of lenders who would gladly talk to you about this strategy. Many offer these shorter loans at lower interest rates, although the rate differential may only amount to one-quarter to one-half percentage point. Still, that's significant as the years go by.

So instead of taking a $100,000, thirty-year loan at 10 percent, contract for a fifteen-year loan at 9½ percent. The monthly payment is $1,044.23. That's $166.55 a month more than the 10 percent loan over thirty years. But if you can scrape up the additional money each month, look at what you'll save.

Over fifteen years, you will pay out principal and interest totalling $187,961.40 (of which $87,961.40 is interest), and the house will be yours. You'll save more than $127,000 in interest payments, plus you will own the house fifteen years earlier.

The second technique that cuts down on the amount of interest you have to pay over the life of the loan and that results in your owning your home free and clear in a short period of time is to increase your monthly payment by just a few dollars each month.

You maintain your 30-year, fixed-rate mortgage at the prevailing interest rate. Check your mortgage to make certain there are no penalties for paying off the loan earlier than required. Then, instead of making only the usual mortgage payment each month, add in an extra $50 or $75 or $100. Make it whatever you can afford; the amounts don't have to be the same each month, so you are not locked in as you would be if you shortened your mortgage by taking out a new, fifteen-year mortgage loan.

You should enclose a note to your bank each month to ensure that your extra payments are applied to the principal, to reduce your outstanding loan balance.

This strategy can result in your owning your home, mortgage-free, years earlier than if you paid the minimum amount each month. How much earlier? That all depends on the amount of extra principal you're paying each month. The more you pay, the faster you reduce the outstanding loan.

However, there is an important fact to note about reducing your interest expense this way. The extra cash payments you make with your regular mortgage checks do not serve to reduce your next month's obligation to send in a check for the full amount called for in the loan documents. For example, say your mortgage payment amounts to $750, but you send in $850. That's fine. The extra $100 will reduce your loan. But the next month, you still must pay at least $750. You don't get to reduce your monthly mortgage payment by the excess you voluntarily sent in previously.

The third technique for reducing your interest outlay is well known in Canada, and some lenders in the States offer it as well. Instead of paying your mortgage with a single check once each month, you pay half your monthly mortgage amount every two weeks. Because there are fifty-two weeks in a year, that amounts to twenty-six half-payments, or thirteen mortgage payments you would make during the year, instead of the usual twelve. Typically, with this type of payment plan, you will pay off the loan in under twenty years and pay much less interest because of the extra mortgage payments you make.

But what if you are already saddled with a thirty-year, fixed-rate mortgage running at 14 percent or more?

You shouldn't be overly anxious to refinance your home mortgage at a lower rate. Bankers love refinancing, even though they may put on a sour face when people inquire about it. That's because taking out a new mortgage means you will be charged a loan origination fee that amounts to at least a couple of percentage points of the amount you are financing, loan application fees, attorney fees, title search expenses, and recording taxes. All those up-front fees can make a dour banker jump for joy.

However, if you can substantially lower your mortgage interest rate, and thereby cut your monthly payment, you should probably grab the chance. You have to work the numbers. Compare the amount you are paying now with the amount you will pay under the refinancing. Then determine the fees you will have to pay in order to refinance. Next determine the number of months it will take for you to recoup the cost in the form of lower finance charges.

For example, if you refinance, you may cut your monthly mortgage expense by $150, but the refinancing expense comes to $3,600. Dividing the $150 into $3,600, you'll find that it will take twenty-four months to break even. If you expect to remain in the house for that long, then refinancing makes sense. But if you expect to be transferred, or will want to move before the cost is recovered, then do not refinance the mortgage.

There are two trouble spots that you need to be aware of when you consider refinancing an existing mortgage.

The IRS says that the points charged by a lender when you refinance a loan are not immediately deductible, but rather have to be taken ratably over the years. If you should sell prior to paying off the loan, you can take the balance of the points that have not been deducted. Say you are refinancing $80,000, and have to pay four points, or $3,200 over the next 25 years. You will be allowed to deduct only $128 a year in additional mortgage interest. If you sell after 10 years (having deducted $1,280), you will be allowed to deduct the remaining $1,920 in the year of sale.

Congress has created a potential problem for those who refinance their existing mortgages. By law, you are not permitted to refinance more than the original price of the residence plus the cost of improvements you have made to it over the year, except in certain specified circumstances. If you borrow more, the interest you pay on the excess will not be deductible. That shouldn't bother too many people, but it does bear watching.

# LESSON 37

## *Tax Breaks of a Business at Home*

Running a business, full- or part-time, out of your home generates a multitude of tax benefits. When you work out of your home, you can claim thousands of dollars worth of tax-deductible expenses that are otherwise unavailable to you.

Your home is your castle. It is also the source of valuable tax breaks when you operate a business out of it.

However, we must warn you. The rules can be complicated. You'll have to file a Schedule C to report your business income and claim your business expenses.

Everyone who owns a home can deduct the full amount of the interest paid on the mortgage loan as well as the real estate taxes paid to the local governments. You don't have to be in business for that.

But if you consult on the side, give piano lessons, write articles, or conduct any of a multitude of other pursuits in your home or apartment, many additional tax breaks become available to you.

In this lesson, we are only going to discuss those tax benefits directly related to the residence. For some of the other advantages of working for yourself, see Lesson 48, "How to Be Your Own Boss."

When you operate a business out of your home, you have to calculate the percentage of business use of the home. You do that by noting the number of square feet that you use for business and dividing that into the total number of square feet in the house. Or you can divide the number of rooms you use for business into the number of rooms in the place. The choice is yours.

Once you know that percentage, you can apply it to many different expenses you incur in your business.

If you own your home, apply the percentage to your mortgage interest and real estate taxes. The business portion is deducted on your Schedule C, and the remaining portion is deducted on your Schedule A.

Apply the percentage of business use to your utility bills, including gas, electric, water, sewage, and oil. Don't use the percentage on your personal telephone bill. With an at-home business, you're better off having a separate business line. The price of a personal line is not tax-deductible. However, if you make long-distance business calls, they are tax-deductible no matter what line they are made on. If you pay homeowner's assessments, use the same percentage when you figure your tax deductions.

The cost of cleaning your home office is tax-deductible. So is what you pay for upkeep and repairs. If you have your home painted, deduct the business percentage. Almost any cost associated with the general maintenance of the home becomes a partial business deduction. A percentage of the cost for repairs to the roof and furnace are legitimate business tax deductions.

It doesn't matter how many hours you work at your sideline business. Whether it's four or forty, the deductions remain the same. The business certainly does not have to generate the major portion of your income, even though some years ago the Internal Revenue Service (IRS) said that it did. Fortunately, the IRS was overruled by Congress on this point.

There's an important rule associated with claiming a deduction for maintaining an office in your home. The office must be used regularly and on an exclusive basis in order for the tax deductions to stand. Running an operation from the dining room table or sewing room won't qualify. It's best to have the basement or a spare bedroom set up for business.

The rules governing the depreciation deduction for the use of your home for business purposes are tedious. First, determine the price you paid for the house, including improvements. Let's say that comes to $100,000. Next, pinpoint the date you acquired the place, not when you first turned it into a business location.

If you bought your house prior to 1981, the depreciation system you must use is to divide the price of the house into anywhere from twenty-five to forty years, depending on your determination of the condition of the property. Say you use twenty-five years. That would result in a $4,000-per-year depreciation deduction if the house was used 100 percent for business. But in our example, only 15 percent of the house is used for business purposes, so the depreciation deduction would amount to $600.

If you bought your house between and including January 1, 1981, and March 15, 1984, you'll use the accelerated depreciation method allowed by law, where you write off the price of the house over fifteen years. The first year, your depreciation deduction was 12 percent, dropping a bit each year under the precise formula set out by law.

If you bought after March 15, 1984, and before May 9, 1985, the depreciation period is eighteen years, and the first year's depreciation was 9 percent, based on the revised statute.

New real estate purchased after May 8, 1985, and before 1987, is depreciated over nineteen years. The percentage for the first year is 8.8. That means a $1,320 deduction.

And if you bought the house in 1987 or later, you have to depreciate it over 27.5 years using the straight-line method of depreciation. That means you get to write off 3.65 percent times 15 percent each year. In this example, that comes to $546. All of these are great incentives for operating a going business out of your home.

We must warn you that the IRS doesn't approve of people operating at-home businesses. It feels that people are cheating here, trying to illegally deduct personal expenses. So it asks on Schedule C if you are deducting expenses for operating a business out of your home. Respond honestly. You have nothing to fear as long as you have the records to back up your deductions, and by following our advice, you do.

Most at-home businesses operate on a shoestring, at least in the beginning. One year you make a profit, while the next year you spend more than you bring in. The tax law has a special rule to cover this situation. You should show a profit in at least three out of five consecutive years in order to claim any tax losses you have with your business. (Through 1986, you only needed to be profitable in two out of five years.) Unless you're profitable, the IRS may say you are really engaged in a personal hobby. And personal expenses are not tax-deductible. If you are profitable, the IRS can't argue that point.

That rule has a far-reaching effect on the tax breaks for operating a business at home. Essentially, it says that you can write off your depreciation deduction so long as it does not reduce your business profits to below zero. You can deduct your operating expenses, including utilities. But when it comes to depreciation, the amount you claim cannot result in a business loss.

So list your business income. Hopefully, you entered into the business to make money, not to lose it. Then deduct your operating expenses, the business share of utilities, mortgage interest, and real estate taxes. Then use your depreciation to offset any profit you may still have.

# JULY

## *Affording College* and *Tax Deductible Vacations*

By planning ahead and taking advantage of strategies that
save on taxes and tap sources of aid, you can ease the
college bite.

Whether you work for yourself or for someone else, the tax
law allows plenty of room for a combined business trip and
vacation.

 *To Do*

- Monthly budget
- Make plans to meet your child's (children's) education
  expenses (see page 163)
- Buy "Don't Miss Out: The Ambitious Student's Guide to
  Financial Aid" (see page 170)

# *Paying for College*

Costs are up and aid is tight, but you can ease the bite by planning ahead.

For the 1986–87 school year, a year at Northwestern University cost $16,175. The University of Virginia cost $6,150 for a Virginia resident, $9,320 for a student from out of state. A veteran high school guidance counselor expresses a view that he hears every day from anxious parents: "The way costs are going up, colleges rank with hospitals."

At the same time, federal money for college scholarships, tuition loans, and work-study programs has not kept up with demand. The formula that determines eligibility for Guaranteed Student Loans and other forms of help excludes many middle-income families, even though their checkbooks tell them that they can't afford college bills. Tax-saving devices have helped many parents finance college for their children, but Congress has narrowed these options in the name of tax reform.

Two laws enacted by Congress in late 1986 re-drew the playing field for the expensive and complicated game of financing college education.

First, the new tax law cuts out some tax-saving devices, narrows others, and makes scholarship and fellowship grants taxable to the extent they exceed the basic costs of tuition and course fees. The tax law also phases out the deduction of interest paid on student and other personal loans.

Second, a substantial overhaul of the Higher Education Act, the law that lays out the rules for federal aid to colleges and college students, will increase the amount a student can receive in grants and loans, but requires all applicants for Guaranteed Student Loans to undergo a "needs test." The needs test is a standard accounting procedure that determines how much a family must pay out of its own pocket before the student can get a subsidized loan. In the past, families with incomes of $30,000 or less could get aid without taking the needs test.

Nevertheless, families that plan ahead and do their homework can still save on taxes while saving toward college, and can still tap bountiful sources of college aid. No matter how vast your wealth, you are throwing money away if you simply pay the bursar's bills every semester. College financial help comes in three kinds, and only one of them is slanted to assist the needy. Indeed, the other two work best for families that have extra income, idle savings, or a business of their own, however small.

The first category covers scholarships, loans, and work-study programs. The second includes gifts, trusts, and other devices that cut your taxes while building savings for your children's education. The third is a sweat-equity system, with your children doing the sweating. Don't pick just one approach; the more sources you can tap, the less you will be encumbered by college costs and the less faint you will feel when your son or daughter proudly announces that the next step is graduate school.

Scholarships and student loans come first in paying tuition bills but come last in planning. You can't do much about them until your child is within a couple of years of college, because you won't know before then how much aid is likely to be available or what kind of college your child is likely to attend. This, however, you can count on: if you are as much as humbly well off by middle-class standards, you will have to come up with a significant chunk of your child's college money. So start planning and building college resources while your children are young.

You'll need lots of money. According to the National Center for Education Statistics, a typical private college that now costs $9,020 a year is likely to cost $12,075 five years from now, and $16,160 ten years from now. A typical public university, now pegged at $4,880 a year, is expected to reach $6,530 in five years, $8,740 in ten. Those figures include tuition, fees, books, supplies, room, board, personal expenses, and transportation. Horrendous as the totals appear, they are simply based on annual increases of 6 percent. Unless you are on a fixed income, your salary and investments should keep pace. By following the lessons in this book, you can lock in investment yields that outstrip 6 percent.

*Gifts* provide the simplest and most straightforward way to build a college nest egg while saving on income taxes. Get your baby a Social Security number, start an account under the Uniform Gifts to Minors Act, and tell all the relatives that gifts to little Jenny's college fund are even more welcome than rattles or dolls.

However, gifts are not quite the tax-saving device they used to be. Besides the gift itself, the greatest benefit of gifts to children is that the money earns interest or dividends, taxed to the child, whose tax bracket is usually low or nil.

Under the new tax law a child under fourteen can take advantage of this benefit on only $1,000 a year in interest or dividend income from gift money. Any interest or dividend income above $1,000 is taxed at the parents' tax bracket, which is usually much higher than the child's. Even if the gift is from someone else—say, a grandparent—the interest or dividend income above $1,000 will be taxed at the parents' bracket.

Of course, $1,000 a year is quite a bit. At current interest rates, you could give Jenny between $11,000 and $12,000 and invest it in a high-yield certificate of deposit maturing when she will start college (see Lesson 27 for how to find the highest-yielding CDs), and stay within the $1,000-a-year limitation.

Furthermore, at age fourteen the limitation ends. And in the meantime there is nothing to stop you from using other tax-saving devices for college savings.

One of the best is single-premium whole life insurance, which we describe in Lesson 28. Let's say your child is four years old and you buy, in your name, a $10,000 single-premium whole life policy and let the earnings accumulate. If its yield averages 8 percent, in ten years the policy will be worth $21,589. You won't pay a penny of federal or state income tax on the earnings. Your child will be fourteen, and you can then decide whether to cash in most of the policy and put the money in a CD in your child's name, or keep it in the policy and let the tax-free earnings continue to accumulate until college bills are due.

That's a conservative approach. If you're willing to take on a little risk in exchange for the prospect of a greater payoff, buy your child shares in one of the growth mutual funds that we recommend in Lesson 21, automatically reinvesting all dividends and capital gain distributions. These dividends and distributions don't amount to a whole lot; most of the payoff from a growth mutual fund results from growth in the value of its shares. So a gift of, say, $15,000 won't yield enough in annual income to exceed the $1,000 limit. But in ten years a good growth mutual fund is likely to gain substantially in value. You can cash in the shares any time after your child's fourteenth birthday, and the gain in value will be taxed to your child, at his or her low tax bracket.

Few parents have $15,000 to give all at once, but you can buy mutual fund shares gradually. One excellent growth fund, Twentieth Century Select, accepts deposits of any size, so you could give your child a stake in Wall Street for five bucks.

Once you've given money to a child you can't take it back. After all, reasons the tax collector, you put the dough in her name, and her tax bracket. So if Jenny reaches eighteen and decides to spend her hoard on a BMW rather than a BA, she's legally entitled. If you're leery about turning the money over to your child, stick with single-premium whole life and pay the tuition bills from the policy's tax-free earnings.

*Trusts* used to be a favorite way to keep the college money out of your child's whimsical reach, while accumulating interest or dividends in a tax bracket much lower than yours. But the new tax law kills Clifford and spousal remainder trusts—the two devices that were tailor-made for college money. However, if you established one of these trusts on or before March 1, 1986, hang on to it; the tax advantages of those older trusts are retroactive. But don't add any more money to the trust; if you do the whole trust will lose its tax advantages.

*Work* earns college money and provides the best tax shelter of all, especially if you or your spouse runs a business, even part-time, and can legitimately hire your children. Some parents with small businesses feel qualms about employing eight-year-old Jenny and deducting her wages, but the federal courts decided that issue years ago in the taxpayers' favor. A child who empties the kitchen trash can also stuff envelopes or run a copying machine. You can pay Jenny a fair wage, deductible to your business, and put it in an account toward her college. If your business is not incorporated, you need not pay Social Security tax on wages paid to your children.

If your child has no unearned income, he or she could earn as much as $2,540 in 1987 ($3,000 in 1988 and beyond) without paying a penny of income tax. That's the new standard deduction under the 1986 tax law. The same tax-free total for 1987 can be put together with work income of, say, $1,640, and interest or dividends of $900. Even if your child earns enough money to be taxed, the bracket will be low.

Before the new tax law went into effect, a child could earn more tax-free income because both the child and the parent could list the child as a dependent on both of their federal income tax returns.

That's important, because each exemption was worth $1,080 in 1986 and is worth $1,900 in 1987, $1,950 in 1988 and $2,000 in 1989 and beyond. But the new tax law declares that Jenny cannot take her own exemption if she is eligible to be claimed as a dependent by her parents—and if you support her, she is eligible.

*College aid based on need* starts with a painfully detailed form designed to determine how much you can afford to pay toward your child's college costs and how much your child can chip in. The formula assumes that you can live on the Department of Labor's "low-budget standard"—$12,540 for a family of four. It also assumes that you'll cash in some of your assets, including your house, or borrow against them. The bottom line throws many families into formula shock. Typically, a family of four with income of $52,000 and net assets of $60,000 will be expected to pay $9,420 a year toward college, according to The College Board.

Nevertheless, the aid formula is worth pursuing. By planning ahead, you can increase your eligibility by lowering your assets. Save as much as you can in IRAs, 401(k)s, and other retirement accounts; the assets formula doesn't count retirement savings.

The formula doesn't factor in consumer debt against your net assets, but it does count mortgage debt, so it may pay you to take out a home equity loan and pay off your other debts. The new tax law also favors home equity loans, because interest on home loans remains fully deductible while interest on other kinds of consumer loans gets phased out as a deduction.

Business and farm assets don't count as heavily as personal assets. If you have a business and can legitimately shift some assets onto that side of the ledger, you'll move the formula your way. If you are a knowledgeable real estate investor, consider buying a duplex or an apartment building in Jenny's college town (see Lesson 34). The building will be a business asset, the mortgage will reduce your net worth, and the depreciation and other deductions may sharply reduce your income, assuming you make under $100,000 a year (see Lesson 34). Jenny can live in one of the apartments. To retain your business deductions, she'll have to pay a fair rent, but you can also pay her a fair salary to manage the building, and deduct her salary. All these deductions cut your taxes and also reduce your ability to pay her college expenses, as determined by that pesky formula.

The formula determines how much you should pay, regardless of her college choice. Let's say your firstborn is awaiting word on her applications to Northwestern, Harvard, and a couple of less expensive institutions, and your financial aid form comes back from the College Scholarship Service, which processes these applications, with word that you should be able to pay $6,000 a year. "Jenny," you say, "$6,000 is your limit, especially with your little brother George just a year away from college." You're thinking in reverse: that $6,000 is Jenny's ticket to a more expensive college, because it means that you're expected to pay only the first $6,000, no matter where she enrolls. Aid is supposed to make up the rest. So if Jenny enrolls in a college that costs $6,000 a year, you'll pay the whole $6,000. If she enrolls in a college that costs $16,175 a year, you'll pay $6,000, and the college's financial aid officer will try to come up with the rest, using mostly federal money that is funneled through the colleges.

Moreover, when George enters college a year later, your ability to pay will be divided by the number of children you have in college. So you'll be expected to ante up $3,000 each, with aid making up the rest.

That's if all goes well. Not every college makes up the entire gap between cost and ability to pay, and most aid is in the form of loans and campus job wages, not outright grants. The richer the college, the greater its ability to grant aid. The more a college wants your student, the more willing it may be to structure the aid package so it includes more in grant money and less from loans or campus toil. You can bargain. You can also include with your formula sheet additional information that may move an aid officer to be more generous. For example, if you are contributing to the support of an elderly relative, make sure the college aid officer knows about it.

Andre L. Bell, director of financial aid for Northwestern University in Evanston, Illinois, points out that colleges can cut back on the formula, too, and are not bashful about requesting tax returns and other proof of financial circumstances. "We may make adjustments to the formula analysis, up or down," Bell says. "For example, let's say we have a family whose source of income is from a job in the city, but they have a small farm generating a tax loss— a gentleman farm situation. That may be deductible under the tax system, but it's not reflective of the family's ability to pay." In such a case, Northwestern would scratch the farm losses and boost the amount the family would have to pay for college.

After all that, though, Northwestern, like most other top-ranked schools, fills in the entire gap between cost and ability to pay. In figuring costs, says Bell, Northwestern allows $3,884 for room and board, $465 for books and supplies, and $795 for personal expenses. Tuition for the 1986–87 school year was $11,031, for a total cost of $16,175. In figuring how much the family can pay, Northwestern computes the family's contribution and figures a freshman should chip in $900 from a summer job; that amount increases for upperclassmen.

Let's say your family's contribution is pegged at $6,000. Even if Jenny spends the summer cultivating her tan, Northwestern adds in $900 from her "summer job." That leaves a gap of $9,275. Northwestern will give Jenny a campus job paying her about $1,500 during the school year, at minimum wage. She'll be expected to borrow $1,850 under the federal Guaranteed Student Loan program, which carries an interest rate of only 8 percent, plus an "origination fee" of 5 percent. The remainder will be met with Northwestern grant money. If that still leaves the family short, Northwestern, like many other institutions, has its own loan program, and lends money to parents at the very favorable interest rate of 8¼ percent.

Every college employs its own variations. At the University of Virginia, says Wayne Sparks, director of financial aid, "we inflate the parents' contribution by 15 percent for students from Virginia and by 20 percent for non-Virginians." So if the formula says you can pay $6,000, Virginia will tell you to pay $6,900 if you live in Virginia, or $7,200 if you're from out of state. On the other hand, a freshman is expected to come up with only $700 from summer work, and Virginia will contribute grant money whether or not a student takes out a Guaranteed Student Loan.

If your family is richer in assets than income, you can figure your ability to pay with a different formula based on income only. A family of four with adjusted gross income (AGI) of $60,000 is expected to come up with $9,780; a family of three with AGI of $35,000 is expected to pay $4,160. If you use that formula, you must renounce all forms of federal aid except Guaranteed Student Loans.

Under the old law, Guaranteed Student Loans were limited to $2,500 a year. The new law raises the limit to $2,625 a year for freshmen and sophomores; $4,000 a year for juniors, seniors, and, for those who need five years to graduate, for the fifth year of undergraduate school; and $7,500 a year for graduate students. In total, an undergraduate can borrow as much as $17,250. A graduate student can pile up GSL debts totaling $54,750, counting loans for both undergraduate and graduate work.

The student does not have to begin repaying the loan until six months after finishing college. The interest rate is 8 percent for the first four years of repayment, 10 percent thereafter. Eight percent is a favorable interest rate, but not as favorable as it used to be when the interest was fully deductible. The Internal Revenue Service counts student loans as consumer debt, just like debt owed on a credit card, and the new tax law allows you to deduct only 65 percent of your consumer loan interest in 1987, decreasing to 40 percent in 1988, 20 percent in 1989, 10 percent in 1990, and none in 1991 and beyond.

Another loan program is called Parent Loans for Undergraduate Students, with an interest rate of 12 percent. That was a favorable interest rate when the program was set up, but it's no longer attractive. You'll pay less on a home equity loan, and get to deduct all the interest.

A superb guide to the maze of college aid offerings, rules, and strategies is *Don't Miss Out: The Ambitious Student's Guide to Financial Aid,* available for $4.75, postpaid, from Octameron Associates, P.O. Box 3437, Alexandria, Virginia 22302.

*Other scholarships and loans* are available to any student, regardless of family wealth. "Nonneed" scholarships, as they are called in academia, are much more plentiful than they were just a few years ago. Many such scholarships are awarded by foundations, corporations, unions, and service organizations like the Elks; others are awarded by the colleges themselves. For example, institutions that now award nonneed scholarships based on academic prowess include Virginia, Johns Hopkins, State University of New York, USC, the University of Colorado, the University of Miami in Florida, the University of Chicago, Purdue, Grinnell College in Iowa, Brandeis, Michigan, Millsaps College in Mississippi, Washington University in St. Louis, Creighton University in Omaha, Temple in Philadelphia, Rutgers, Wake Forest, Miami University in Ohio, the University of Oklahoma, Carnegie-Mellon, Vanderbilt, Rice, Brigham Young, Washington State University, Beloit College in Wisconsin—and literally hundreds of others.

Special talents also are rewarded, notably athletic skills. It's no secret that Indiana and North Carolina, to pick two examples at random, award basketball scholarships to tall men, but it is less well known that Georgetown, Kentucky, Minnesota, Berkeley, and many other institutions offer women's scholarships in swimming, track, volleyball, and other sports.

Whether your talent is drumming or dancing or debating, some organization or college almost surely offers scholarship help, providing you're good enough. Just as high school coaches put their outstanding athletes in touch with the right colleges, the teacher or bandleader who specializes in your skills should know where to steer you and should put in a word on your behalf. Don't be too shy to ask. Even if no scholarship is forthcoming, a skill might help you gain admission to the college of your choice or give you leverage in putting together a favorable package of aid based on need. For example, Harvard and Yale don't grant athletic scholarships, but athletes coveted by their coaches have a leg up in the admissions process.

Your Jenny may wind up with the scholarship clout of an Albert Einstein or a Bo Jackson. Then again, she may choose a college that fails to properly reward her skills. Most children do, and most parents pay. If you do your homework with the same diligence you expect of Jenny, you can build a plan and a nest egg that will pay her way through the right college without crushing the family fortunes. It's time well spent and money well saved.

# LESSON 39

## Combining Personal Vacations with Business Trips, Legally

Combine personal vacations with legitimate business trips and write off the lion's share of the cost. It's not difficult, it's not illegal (despite what you may have heard about the new tax law), and it doesn't matter whether you are self-employed or a salaried employee.

Sitting down to prepare your income tax return in February or March is doubtless not a favorite experience. However, you might find yourself smiling as you think back on those fond memories of one or more restful vacations you took last year and realize that you enjoyed yourself at the expense of the Internal Revenue Service (IRS).

Almost everyone who works for a living can combine tax-deductible business trips with nondeductible personal vacations and write off the biggest part of the cost. All it takes is a little advance planning and knowledge of the old and new tax requirements imposed by the IRS.

We know there are skeptics out there, saying something like "OK, how can a secretary or a retail sales clerk write off a trip?" The answer is by attending office-product and trade shows that are held throughout the country. Sales clerks can attend management meetings and product seminars in their fields. How about a flower vendor? Go to a regional trade show on the latest trends in the business. All it takes is a little creativity to find a meeting associated with your line of work. You don't need a special invitation, but you must be able to afford the price of the trip, room, meals, and meeting.

Once you determine when and where you want to go, brush up on the tax requirements covered in this lesson. If you do, then the deductions are yours for the taking, and it's all perfectly legal. Plus, if you are employed (as opposed to self-employed) and can get your employer to pick up the tab, you can actually enjoy your fun in the sun for free or at least at a very small cost.

The point is that whenever you board a plane for a business meeting, pack the car for a family vacation, or decide to visit relatives or friends while you are out of town, you can rest assured that at least some part of your expenses will be tax-deductible.

Now a word of caution: because the IRS considers this to be an area prone to tax abuse, it has made it its business to closely scrutinize travel and entertainment expenses. However, the fact remains that under the tax laws, regulations, and court decisions, it is quite simple to combine business with pleasure and claim your write-off without being challenged. Just be sure you keep all your records and receipts to verify what you will be claiming on your tax return, including airline tickets, agendas from the meeting, hotel bills, that sort of thing.

Here's a quick rundown on some of the detailed rules to keep in mind.

To qualify for a business deduction, the trip must be for a meeting, convention, or seminar that is directly related to your trade or business. When it is, you can deduct registration fees, travel to and from the meeting, cabs, hotel rooms, most of your meal expenses and most other expenses associated with your attendance at the meeting.

Luxury travel to get there is out. First class air fare is fine, but a cruise ship is not. If you sail, you will be restricted to only twice the per diem travel cost in the U.S.

Conventions on cruise ships are still OK, as long as you meet those detailed rules. See your tax advisor before setting sail.

Meals eaten while traveling on business, even convention meals, will only be 80 percent deductible, unless your firm reimburses you for the cost. Same for entertainment expenses. And to even qualify for the limited deduction, you have to be having business discussions either during, immediately preceding or following the meal or entertainment. The only exception to this is when you're eating alone. Congress doesn't think it wise to force you to talk to yourself in a room full of diners.

When your firm reimburses your cost, you have a wash, and the firm deducts only 80 percent of the cost.

Banquet meals are an exception when the meals are part of the program, more than half the people are from out of town, there are more than 40 people attending the meeting, and there is a dinner speaker. In that case, the full price of the meal is tax deductible.

Here's a typical situation. You decide to attend a trade show or convention, a management seminar, or a similar meeting. You pay the registration fees, program charges, airline tickets, cabs, meals, lodging, and even some entertainment expenses for colleagues. There's no tax question, assuming you have kept receipts.

One note of caution: investment seminars and educational travel are out. Period. Don't even think about trying to deduct costs associated with them. The new tax law expressly prohibits it.

When you attend a legitimate business-related convention, remember to have some fun. There's no rule that says you have to be cooped up in a stuffy room twenty-four hours a day, considering some boring business subject. After spending six to eight hours a day working and attending meetings and conferences, go ahead and shoot a round of golf, lounge around the pool or on the beach, play a little tennis. You may want to go fishing. That's perfectly acceptable.

The key tax rule to keep in mind as you plan your business-vacation trip is that the primary purpose of your trip must be business-related. This means you must spend a majority of your days away from home on business rather than personal pursuits. If you do, you can write off your transportation costs to and from the meeting as well as all business-related expenses you have while attending the business convention.

So how does this help with a personal vacation? Just tack on a couple of personal days around the business portion of the trip. For example, say you attend a seven-day business meeting. Afterward, you take a side trip for another five days to visit with family and friends. Then you return home. The transportation costs to and from the convention site are tax-deductible, and so are all the meeting expenses. The cost of your side trip, while not deductible since it is a personal expense, does not wipe out the deductions for the business portion of the trip.

If your business meeting is only three days and you then vacation an additional five days after that, you will violate the "primarily for business" rule. In that case, only your actual out-of-pocket convention expenses such as room, meals, and other costs can be written off. You will lose your transportation expenses.

Can you take your spouse along with you on business trips and legitimately deduct the extra expenses? Certainly, if you plan carefully. The IRS traditionally dislikes it when you deduct your spouse's expenses. But the tax collector has OK'd them when the spouse contributes materially to the business meeting. Attending simply to keep you on schedule, write memos, and attend formal receptions is not enough. But when official functions are called for, you shouldn't have any problem. For example, if you operate your own small, at-home business and your spouse is an officer and paid employee, attendance by both of you at a trade show will be acceptable to the IRS.

In fact, it is possible to take along your entire family, although not for free, but certainly at a reduced cost. For example, say you have a business convention coming up at a nice vacation spot. The kids will be out of school during that time, and your spouse can get off work. If you fly, the price of your ticket is deductible; the price of theirs is not. If you drive, the entire cost of gas, oil, maintenance, and so forth is deductible because it costs no more to operate a car with one in it than with four or five.

You can deduct only the cost of a single-occupancy room. Still, you get a great deal. A single may cost $100, while four in the room comes to $160 ($20 extra per person). Even better, stay in a "suites-only" hotel. That way all of the room charge is deductible. The cost of your meals is at least 80 percent deductible; the cost of theirs is not.

While you attend to business, the rest of the family can vacation. You can join them at the end of the day and when the convention adjourns. It's a terrific tax opportunity because you can deduct the lion's share of transportation and room expenses.

From a tax standpoint, one of the easiest and safest methods of planning a tax-deductible meeting or convention is to structure it around your small business. The tax law makes no distinction between the giants of industry and little "mom-and-pop" operations. All are treated equally under the tax law. If you have your own small business, you can attend your own annual meeting just like a General Motors or an IBM. If you want to take the board of directors to the Greenbrier in West Virginia or The Breakers in Florida, go ahead. Your annual meeting expenses are simply a cost of doing business and are tax-deductible.

Salaried employees actually have a relatively easy time writing off their travel and entertainment expenses. You incur your expense and put in for reimbursement. When your receipts are accepted by your employer, you'll get a check. If you have expenses that exceed what your employer will pay, you get to deduct the excess.

Self-employed individuals don't get reimbursed. The cost of their business trips is borne by their business and affects the bottom line. Because the IRS is concentrating on small-business taxpayers and is certain to question business travel and entertainment expenses claimed on those returns, you must keep all of your records and receipts. With them, chances are you will have no problem with the IRS's accepting your deductions.

Keep in mind the way your deductions affect your taxes. When a self-employed person attends a business convention and has to pay $4,000 in transportation, meeting, room, meals, and other expenses for the week, that means a $2,880 out-of-pocket expense, assuming a 28 percent tax bracket. A salaried employee, on the other hand, will usually find that the employer will pick up most of the cost of attending a business convention. And once you turn in your receipts to the company's accountant, you won't hear any more about it. The IRS says if you can substantiate your expenses to your employer, that's good enough for the tax agency.

Feel free to plan your personal vacation around a business trip. Take your spouse and children along. Just make certain that you spend more time on business than on pleasure and that you save your receipts. Then, at tax time, you can fondly remember those carefree days while you write off a sizable chunk of your expenses.

# AUGUST

## *Insurance*

Buy insurance only to pay for contingencies that you could not afford to handle out-of-pocket. For support of your loved ones, buy the cheapest and most straightforward kind of life insurance. To pay bills if you are unable to work, consider disability insurance. For your car, house, and activities, buy plenty of liability coverage. Choose health insurance that will cover catastrophes.

 *To Do*

- Monthly budget
- Tax return due August 15 if you filed for extension
- Buy the mutual fund issue of Forbes Magazine (late August/ early September)
- Call Insurance Information and check out the best insurance rates around the country (see page 179)
- Order free copy of National Insurance Consumer Organization "Buyer's Guide" booklet (see page 185)

# *The Best, Easiest, and Cheapest Life Insurance*

Don't buy whole life insurance or universal life or any other kind of "cash-value" life insurance. Buy annual renewable term life and find the best deal by calling (800) 472-5800.

Annual renewable term, or ART, is far and away the cheapest and most sensible kind of life insurance. If you have an insurance agent who tells you to buy "cash-value" insurance of one kind or another, you should resist, as he is wrong.

Cash-value life comes in many forms. Whole life and universal life are the most common terms used to describe this kind of insurance. Whatever a sales rep calls it, it's a curious hybrid—a combination of savings, which you can cash in later in life, and life insurance, which pays off when you die. That makes about as much sense as combining savings with, say, your electric bill. Would you like to pay an additional $50 a month on your electric bill to build up a savings account? We wouldn't, and we wouldn't want to save through our life insurer, either. We'd rather keep our savings separate. (The one exception is the unusual investment called "single-premium whole life," which we discussed in Lesson 28.)

ART includes no savings or other frills; your survivors collect only when you die. Premiums rise annually, because the older you are, the more likely you will die that year. Premiums for most cash-value policies are level, year after year. That sounds good, but it means that you pay more in your younger years, when you can least afford it, in order to keep premiums level in your older years, when you can better afford it.

Because of the savings contribution that's part of the premium, cash-value life insurance costs a whole lot more than plain term insurance. Let's say you're a male nonsmoker, thirty-five years old. You want $250,000 of life insurance coverage—a sensible amount, assuming your dependents will need income after your death.

You can call Northwestern Mutual, perhaps the best of the cash-value life insurers, and buy NW Mutual's best policy, called Select 100 Life. The premium will be $3,585 a year (the premiums we quote here may have changed a little by the time you read this). The premium won't rise, and the policy will accumulate cash value.

Or you can do what we recommend: call Insurance Information at (800) 472-5800 and ask for the cheapest ART policy for someone of your age and sex. Insurance Information provides a truly superb and innovative service. It gathers ART rates from dozens of insurers and files them in a computer. For $50, charged to your Visa or MasterCard, it runs a computer search for the lowest ART rates for you and sends you printouts from the four or five lowest-cost insurance companies. If at least one of these deals doesn't save you money on your life insurance, you get your $50 back.

We tried it, for our mythical thirty-five-year-old nonsmoker male, and Insurance Information came through with rates from two highly rated insurers. Security Mutual Life quoted $207 the first year, scaling up to $327 the fifth year, at age thirty-nine. Premiums for the first five years totaled $1,352. Bankers National Life quoted a high first-year premium of $317 but then dropped the premium to $202 the second year, scaling up to $285 the fifth year, at age thirty-nine. Premiums for the first five years totaled $1,865.

That's for the same $250,000 coverage that would cost you *$3,585 every year* from Northwestern Mutual. This is not a misprint. For the same insurance coverage, the difference in cost is immense. And don't forget, we're bending over backward; NW Mutual is a fine company. You could buy cash-value life elsewhere and pay a lot more.

What could be better than an insurance choice that you can make with one phone call—a free phone call, at that? Even if you already have ART and know that you bought the cheapest policy available, it's worthwhile to check with Insurance Information every couple of years. Life insurance is a very competitive business. Companies crowd each other with premium cuts, and last year's best buy may no longer be competitive.

If you have owned a cash-value policy for five years or more, check whether it is a "participating" policy, meaning one under which you, as a policyholder, participate in the profits of the insurance company. If it is, your old policy may be worth keeping. If not, and for any additional life insurance needs, switch to ART.

# *Paying the Bills if You're Disabled*

For many people, disability insurance is more important than life insurance.

Here's the case for disability insurance, bluntly stated by James H. Hunt of the National Insurance Consumer Organization: "If you're dead, you're gone, and you have no more expenses. If you're disabled, that's not the case, and your care can be quite expensive."

It's easy to decide whether you or your spouse needs disability coverage. Ask yourself this question: If you or your spouse could no longer work, would you need to replace that lost income? Remember, too, that disability is not an all-or-nothing thing. You might need to insure against a partial disability that would cut your income, perhaps by forcing you to work fewer hours or making you switch to an occupation that pays less.

Disability insurance goes hand in hand with life insurance; both are designed to protect against loss of income. Some people need one but not the other. For example, few singles need life insurance, because no one is dependent on them. But self-supporting singles should seriously consider disability insurance. If they're laid up, who is going to support them?

It may be hard to imagine an illness or accident that would keep you away from work for, say, three or four months. Sudden death seems more likely. Yet according to a survey published by the Social Security Administration in 1982, 6 percent of adult Americans are classified as disabled, meaning that they are unable to return to work.

Many working couples decide against disability coverage on the grounds that if one spouse could no longer work, the other's paycheck would be enough. But in many cases, the disability of one spouse forces the other to curtail his or her work in order to care for the ailing partner.

Life insurance usually pays a lump sum at death, but disability insurance provides monthly checks, like the paychecks they are designed to replace.

Look first to your employer. Many fringe benefit packages include disability coverage. If your group policy pays insufficient benefits or provides payments for only, say, two to five years, as many do, you can buy a private policy that would supplement those benefits or pick up when the group policy runs out. Social Security also provides benefits, but not until you have been laid up for five full months and then only if you are unable to work at anything. For example, a doctor who suffered a stroke but was able to work half-days as a janitor would not qualify for Social Security disability benefits. For those who do get them, monthly Social Security disability benefits average about $475 for a single disabled worker, $893 for a disabled worker with a family.

Private disability insurers will cover up to 60 percent of your work income—no more. That's partly because disability payments aren't taxable. Kenneth A. McClure, an assistant vice president of USAA Life Insurance Company, told us another reason: "The insurer wants it to be to your advantage to go back to work."

If you have a safe and prestigious white-collar job, you'll probably qualify for the lowest disability premiums. That's largely because white-collar jobs tend to be safer than blue-collar jobs. A roofer, for example, might pay 2½ times as much as a lawyer for the same amount of disability coverage. But another factor is the relative desire to return to work, as reflected in the statistical experience of insurance companies. "We avoid people who have no interest in getting back to work," says Ken McClure. "That includes a low-paid clerk or an unskilled worker, someone who has a boring job."

The best disability policies bar the insurer from canceling the policy or increasing the premium, even if your health goes bad or you change occupations. Insurers offer differing definitions of "disability," so look out for restrictive definitions. Here's a dilly: A few years ago, federal courts took on the case of a man whose policy stipulated that he could collect only if a disability confined him to his home. He suffered a heart attack and eventually began taking walks on the advice of his doctor. The insurer cut off his payments, saying that he was no longer confined to home. Good news: he sued and won.

Connecticut Mutual, one of the best disability insurers, offers two options. The more expensive—known within the trade as "own occupation"—pays full benefits if you can't work at your old job, no matter how much you might earn by switching professions. The other definition is less costly, and we think it's more sensible; payments are based on the amount of income you lose as a result of disability.

Let's say you're thirty-five years old, a professional earning $50,000 a year, and you choose a Connecticut Mutual policy protecting 60 percent of your income, or $30,000. The policy will begin paying after ninety days of disability and continue paying, as long as you are disabled, until age sixty-five. The annual premium is $675.25. (As with other figures in this book, the precise amount may have changed by the time you read this.) For an additional $202.50 a year, you can buy a kind of inflation protection clause that would automatically increase your benefits, after disability, by 5 percent a year. For another $103, you can get the "own occupation" option, and for yet another $148.50, you can buy coverage that will pay you until death rather than cutting off at age sixty-five. Connecticut Mutual sells so-called participating policies, meaning that you, as a policyholder, participate in the company's profits. Your share of those profits is called dividends and is used to reduce your premiums. After the second year, dividends will reduce the annual premiums by about 10 percent.

Premiums are the same for men and women and are level, year after year. The older you are when you buy the policy, the higher your risk of disability, and the higher the premium. At forty-five, the same coverage would cost $1,033 a year, plus $243 for the 5 percent inflation clause, $163.50 for "own occupation" coverage, and $229.50 for payments until death.

We advise against the "own occupation" rider. We also consider the inflation coverage too expensive. The rider providing payments until death is worth considering, although it, too, is costly.

Independent insurance agents sell Connecticut Mutual policies and also handle excellent disability policies offered by Maccabees Mutual Life, National Life of Vermont, Provident Life and Accident, Union Mutual, and United Life and Accident. USAA Life sells its excellent disability policies by phone and mail only; call (800) 531-8000. Each policy differs at least a little bit in coverage, so it's hard to say which is the best buy.

It's no fun to buy disability or life insurance. Let's finish this on a cheerful note. If you can count on a good level of support from investments or a rich uncle, you probably don't need disability insurance.

# LESSON 42

## *Auto and Other Liability Insurance*

Go heavy on liability, light on other coverage. In comparing rates, start with State Farm.

Let's get right down to it: Good citizens sometimes are the cause of dreadful automobile accidents that kill, cripple, or disfigure others. Victims may collect hundreds of thousands of dollars. That's why you need a whole lot of liability coverage.

On the other hand, if you wreck your own car, how much have you lost? Your insurer won't pay you more than its value; if the car is worth $5,000 but would cost $7,000 to repair, you'll get $5,000. So you might want to do without collision coverage or take a high deductible to cut the premium. The less valuable your car, the less reason to buy collision insurance. But buy comprehensive. It's cheap and covers you in case of theft or damage caused by a falling limb or other accidents unrelated to a collision.

Your risk of liability losses isn't limited to auto accidents. You could bean someone, or your bicycling teenager could knock down a pedestrian. The mail carrier might slip on your sidewalk and break her leg.

We think the wisest buy is a combination of auto liability, homeowner's liability, and a so-called umbrella liability policy, which protects you and your family against liability judgments of any kind. Typically, an insurer will package an auto policy with liability coverage of $300,000 or $500,000, a homeowner's policy with liability coverage of $100,000, and an umbrella liability policy providing $1 million of coverage. The umbrella policy costs $115 to $150 a year. It's well worth it.

We're great admirers of the National Insurance Consumer Organization (NICO), a nonprofit advisory group run by Robert Hunter, a former federal insurance administrator. In picking an auto insurer, NICO recommends that you start with State Farm. Our own experience supports NICO's recommendation. State Farm has a superb record for settling claims quickly and honestly, and since it is the nation's largest auto insurer, you can always find an agent.

(The National Insurance Consumer Organization offers a "Buyer's Guide" booklet on auto insurance and other kinds of insurance. For a free copy, send a stamped, self-addressed envelope to NICO, 121 North Payne Street, Alexandria, Virginia 22314.)

Auto insurance premiums rose 18 percent, on average, during 1985. State Farm is not always the best buy. But it's usually close, and it serves as a benchmark against which you can compare other premiums. If you are an active or retired military officer, check with USAA (United Services Automobile Association) at (800) 531-8858. NICO also recommends Amica Mutual (check your phone book). GEICO ([800] 841-3000) is also worth considering.

# LESSON 43

## *Homeowner's Insurance*

Consider full-replacement coverage for the contents of your home and make sure your valuables are covered.

You should insure your house for 80 percent of the cost of replacing it. That means construction cost, not market value; your yard won't burn, and neither will the foundation. Unless you live miles and miles from the nearest fire station, it's very unlikely that your house will be totally destroyed. So 80 percent of the replacement cost is usually plenty.

If you have, say, an old Victorian house or a slate roof and would want to rebuild your house just as it is, you may want to pay a little extra for a special kind of replacement coverage.

Replacement coverage almost always makes sense for the contents of your house. Ordinary homeowner's policies cover possessions for half as much as the house. If your house would cost $100,000 to rebuild and your policy covers it up to $80,000, your possessions would be covered up to $40,000. That may sound like plenty, but for many families, it is not.

By increasing your premium by about 15 percent, you can insure the contents of your house for the replacement value. It's money well spent, because otherwise, you get only the depreciated value. Say you bought an $800 stereo five years ago. Its present value may be only $400; under a standard policy, that's all you'd get if the stereo were stolen or destroyed. But today, it might cost you $1,000 to replace that stereo. If you have replacement-value coverage, you'd get the full $1,000.

Photograph every room in your house, from every angle, and put the snapshots in your safe-deposit box, with the date noted. That's the only way to recall—and prove—exactly what was lost in a fire or burglary.

If you own a condominium, your condo fee almost surely includes homeowner's coverage—although probably not for the contents of your condo. Check the coverage and, if necessary, buy insurance for your possessions. If you rent a home, the owner is responsible for insuring the building, but you'll need insurance to cover your possessions.

If you own valuables, you probably should buy policy riders, or floaters, to cover them, because homeowner's policies severely limit coverage of—among other items—furs, jewelry, cash, bank notes, gold and silver, guns, boats, trailers, stamp and coin collections, and business papers. The riders are not unreasonably priced. For example, most standard homeowner's policies cover $2,500 worth of sterling silverware. A rider adding another $2,500 of coverage costs about $10 a year.

As with automobile collision coverage, a homeowner's deductible higher than the standard $250 makes sense, because it cuts your insurance premium significantly. By increasing the deductible to $1,000, you can cut your homeowner's premium by 25 to 30 percent.

Also as with auto insurance, we recommend State Farm for homeowner's coverage; use State Farm's rates as a benchmark for comparisons with other insurers. Lest you think you can wisely use State Farm for all your insurance needs, sorry, but it ain't so. In most cases, State Farm's rates for life and disability insurance are too high.

# LESSON 44

## *Health Insurance, Even between Jobs*

If you don't have good health insurance through your job or your spouse's job, look into an HMO.

Group health insurance provides the best coverage at the best rates. A "group" can be as small as two or three people, so no matter how small your office, check with Blue Cross–Blue Shield and other insurers about group rates. A note of caution: be wary of health insurance plans offered through large organizations such as auto clubs. These group policies appeal mostly to people who can't get insurance elsewhere. As a result, the groups tend to be high-risk people, and the premiums tend to be very high.

Whether you're shopping on your own or for a small group, look into HMOs—short for health maintenance organizations. An HMO has drawbacks; some are sterile and crowded clinics, and in some, the turnover of doctors is high. But many are solid, dependable operations. Some HMOs are "without walls"—you choose from a list of subscribing private physicians and hospitals.

HMOs have strong economic advantages and also offer time-saving convenience. Blue Cross–Blue Shield and other health insurers include a deductible in their policies and, in most cases, also require "coinsurance." That means that you pay 20 percent of every doctor's bill. With private health insurance, you have to save medical bills, file claim forms, and decipher the replies you get from the insurance office. With most HMOs, your premium covers all your care, and you never have to file a claim form.

If you have to buy health insurance on your own and choose not to join an HMO, check into Blue Cross–Blue Shield. Other insurers recommended by the National Insurance Consumer Organization include American Republic of Des Moines, Iowa ([515] 245-2000); Washington National of Evanston, Illinois ([312] 570-5500); and two firms that have offices in major cities—Kemper, and Mutual of Omaha. If you are fifty or older and for some reason cannot buy health insurance at a reasonable price, join the American Association for Retired Persons—the dues are a whopping five bucks a year, for you and your spouse—and look into AARP's health coverage through Prudential. It's not a top-of-the-line policy, because hospitalization payments are limited to $100 a day. But no AARP member can be refused coverage, and among "club" policies, the AARP's stands out. For AARP membership information, phone (202) 872-4700.

Avoid "cancer" policies and all other single-illness coverage. You want coverage for any and all ailments, with extremely high limits. It doesn't much matter whether your first few hundred dollars of medical bills are covered, so you might want to take a high deductible in exchange for a lower premium. But it matters a lot whether your policy would pay, say, $500,000 in case you were hit with a catastrophic illness.

Blue Cross–Blue Shield charges the same premium regardless of sex or age and has just one "family" rate, whether your family consists of two people or a dozen. In effect, that means younger people, who use less health care, subsidize older people, who use more; smaller families subsidize larger ones; and men subsidize women, since, on average, a woman's health-care costs are higher than a man's. If you are young—particularly a young man—or if your family is small, you might be better off with an insurer that charges premiums based on age, sex, and size of family. One such company worth checking is Washington National ([312] 570-5500). Policies such as those sold by Washington National also are handy "fillers" if you need coverage while between jobs.

# LESSON 45

## *Insurance to Skip*

Don't waste your money on credit life insurance, flight insurance, or car rental insurance.

When you borrow money, lenders often try to sell you credit life insurance; in the case of a home loan, it's called mortgage life insurance. These policies pay off the loan if you die. But why make your creditor the beneficiary of your life insurance? Instead, make sure you have enough term life coverage so your survivors will be able to handle debts as well as other needs.

Flight insurance, sold at airports, is even more foolish. You're insuring your life against one risk. Anyway, survivors of air-crash victims commonly get six-figure settlements from the airline, whether or not the victims carried flight insurance.

Just as you don't want to insure your life against only one cause of death, you shouldn't insure your health against only one disease. Buy term life insurance and health insurance with broad coverage. Avoid cancer insurance, muggers' insurance, and other single-illness policies.

When you rent a car, you're offered additional insurance coverage. You can probably skip it. If you have State Farm insurance on your own car, the same coverage extends to cars you rent. Most other insurers provide the same extension.

For heaven's sake, don't buy pet insurance. We love our pets, too. The Strassels family has a golden retriever and two parakeets and cares for a flock of ducks on a pond nearby. The Meads dote on two cats. But veterinary treatment isn't so expensive as to warrant health insurance for animals. You're not going to take your cat in for a CAT scan or your dog for plastic surgery. You buy insurance to cover costs that you could not afford on your own, not to pay every bill that comes along.

With all the insurance coverage you do need, aren't you glad to find some kinds you can skip?

# SEPTEMBER

## *Borrowing Wisely*

Lots of people consider debt a pleasure, because of the tax deduction. We think it is a pain. We also consider most credit cards unnecessarily expensive, and recommend Visa and MasterCards that offer unusually favorable terms.

 *To Do*

- Monthly budget
- Second estimated tax payment due September 15
- Third tax review session, early September (see page 48)
- Call BankCard Holders of America for best credit card rates (see page 194)
- If you need to borrow money, check out alternative sources of loans, such as your whole life insurance policy. Consider joining a credit union.
- Start saving toward your retirement account contribution to be made in January

# *Right and Wrong Credit Cards*

Plain Visa and MasterCards provide the most versatile buy. Interest rates, annual fees, and other terms vary all over the lot. We've done some bargain hunting.

Americans are getting blitzed with advertisements for credit cards promising new and distinctive features. But you'll save time and money by sticking to two or three credit card accounts. You'll also save by paying your bills on time, because credit card interest is no longer fully deductible.

For most of us, the best and most versatile credit card is a basic Visa or MasterCard. Both are accepted at some 4 million establishments in the United States and overseas. You can use either card at banks, here and in some cities abroad, to get a cash advance or to buy traveler's checks.

Visa Cards and MasterCards are issued by thousands of banks, and terms vary widely. Most people don't think of bargain hunting when it comes to credit cards, and many banks take advantage of this free lunch. They charge high interest rates and high annual fees, allow very short grace periods or none at all, and severely limit your credit line. (The "grace period" is the number of days you get to pay your bill before interest is charged. The "credit line" is the total balance you're allowed to run up.)

But some banks are aggressively pursuing business by offering better terms. If your bank and others in your city don't offer competitive deals, look out of state. You handle your credit card bills by mail anyway, so there's no particular advantage in limiting yourself to a Visa or MasterCard from a local bank.

When we wrote this, credit card interest rates varied from 10.5 percent to over 20 percent and annual fees from zero—that's right, no annual fee—to $30 or more. Some banks offer no grace period at all; you're charged interest from the day the charge is posted to your account, even though you haven't yet been billed. Credit lines ranged from $250 to $10,000.

All these terms are important. A high credit line enables you to use your card for big charges and long vacations. A grace period of twenty or twenty-five days lets you take full advantage of your credit card. For example, you might charge a nice meal on, say, September 15, get billed for it October 10, and have until October 30 to pay—in all, six weeks of interest-free "float." Look out for banks that advertise a low interest rate but tell you only in the small print that you get no grace period at all. Always ask banks for a complete list of terms.

For the information that follows, we're indebted to two bargain hunters. Congressman Charles E. Schumer, Democrat of New York, became outraged at high interest rates and asked his staff to survey banks and release a list of those that charged relatively low rates of interest on Visa and MasterCard balances. A consumer group, BankCard Holders of America ([202] 543-5805), searched for banks that charge the lowest annual fees. Shown below is the best of both lists. If you pay your bills on time, go with a bank that charges no annual fee. If you pay your bills late, opt for a bank that charges a low interest rate. We have to throw in our usual caveat: banks may have changed their terms since we wrote this.

Unless your needs are unusual, we don't consider the so-called travel and entertainment cards a good buy. An American Express card costs $45 a year, a Diners Club card costs $55, and an American Express Gold Card costs $65. To be sure, these cards have certain advantages over Visa and MasterCard. They impose no credit limit and charge no interest; you're supposed to pay in full every month. They offer extra services that can be helpful while you're traveling.

But not even American Express is accepted at nearly as many establishments as are Visa and MasterCard. For a prestigious card with a high credit limit and the same kind of extras that go with an American Express Gold Card, consider the Visa Gold Card offered by Union National Bank, P.O. Box 1541, Little Rock, Arkansas 72203 ([800] 351-9125). It costs $35 a year. After you're billed, you get twenty days to pay. Only then is interest charged, at an annual rate of 11 percent. The credit limit is $5,000 or more, depending on your income.

You may also want credit cards from particular stores and oil companies. Stores and oil companies typically charge no credit card fee, so obtaining their cards is painless. But the more credit cards you use, the more bills you will have to pay, and the more monthly deadlines you will have to keep track of to avoid interest charges. Many stores and service stations accept Visa and MasterCard.

Keep it simple. One Visa or MasterCard account with a high credit limit can take the place of a half-dozen separate accounts.

| Bank | Annual fee | Interest rate | Grace period | Maximum credit line |
|---|---|---|---|---|
| Imperial Savings Association<br>P.O. Box 23525<br>San Diego, California 92123<br>(Californians phone [800]<br>542-6209. Out-of-staters<br>phone [800] 345-3263.)<br>Type of card: Visa | None | 19.8% | 25 days | $10,000 |
| Simmons First National Bank<br>P.O. Box 7009<br>Pine Bluff, Arkansas 71601<br>([501] 541-1000)<br>Type of card: Visa or<br>MasterCard | $22.50 | 10.5% | 25 days | $ 4,000 |

# LESSON 47

## How to Borrow and Why Paying Interest Is a Burden Despite the Tax Deduction

You shouldn't borrow unless you have to. And when you do, look for nontraditional sources. Often, they provide the best deals.

Most people feel uncomfortable, perhaps even a bit embarrassed, when they have to approach someone for a loan. You have to justify to somebody else why he should trust you with his money while you pay off your loan. It doesn't matter if it's a friend, relative, or stranger (like a bank officer). What's more, the interest rates these days are so high that they resemble what loan sharks used to charge, even though they have dropped from the even higher levels of just a few years ago.

Borrowing is expensive. When you fail to pay off your credit card balance each month, the annual interest rate charged by most banks is in the 18 to 20 percent range. The rate on personal loans is in the double digits. While we are preparing this book, automobile manufacturers are offering great deals on auto loans, but that's a promotion and is likely to end; when it does, car loans will be back to 11 percent or more. And of course, housing loans are still near 10 percent.

All in all, that's a pretty stiff price to pay for the use of money, especially when inflation has been held in check for the past couple of years. Over the past three years, inflation has stabilized at below 4 percent a year.

You may argue that interest rates are not as bad as they seem at first glance, that you enjoy a tax deduction for the interest you pay on that car loan, to your credit card company, and to the bank. That's true. You do enjoy a tax deduction, but it's limited.

The Tax Reform Act makes 1986 the last year that you can fully deduct the amount of consumer interest you pay out on credit card balances, bank and student loans, auto financing and other types of personal installment debt. In 1987, only 65 percent of that interest will be deductible, 40 percent in 1988, 20 percent in 1989, and 10 percent in 1990. After that, the deduction for consumer interest is repealed. Interest you pay on a home mortgage as well as what you pay on a mortgage covering a second or vacation home is fully tax deductible, this year and forever more.

Say that you paid $500 in credit card interest in 1986. If you find yourself in a 38 percent tax bracket, that means you will enjoy a tax benefit of $190. That's not $500. That $500 expense still costs you a cool $310 no matter how you try to justify it. In other words, you get a tax break of 38 cents on the dollar. But you have to foot the other 62 cents on your own. That's a steep price to pay.

It gets steeper in 1987. Say that you pay another $500 in interest, but now you are in the 28 percent tax bracket, thanks to tax reform. What's more, only 65 percent of the interest you pay is deductible. So, the $500 interest payment is only worth a $325 deduction, and, because of the 28 percent tax bracket, is really worth only a $91 tax benefit. You pay $500, and the IRS pays $91. That's not a very good deal.

What's more, over 40 percent of all taxpayers are not allowed any benefit whatsoever from their interest payments because they file one of the short income tax forms. To enjoy any tax benefit for interest paid out during the year, you have to file the long form, 1040.

We recommend that you avoid borrowing unless it's absolutely necessary. The price is just too high. You're better off saving your money at 6 to 10 percent interest and paying cash for your purchases than you are financing at 18 to 20 percent.

There are, to be sure, situations where borrowing is too good a deal to pass up. It makes good sense to use other people's money interest-free rather than withdrawing your own savings that are drawing interest. For example, on many credit cards, you can enjoy thirty to forty-five days' or more free use of the store's or bank's money. You charge your purchase and pay off the balance when you get your bill, with no interest charge assessed against you.

In late 1986, some automakers were touting car loans of under 3 percent. When you can borrow from someone else at a rate that is lower than what you are earning on your savings, by all means, take the lender up on the offer. However, don't get caught up in the advertising. Work through the numbers. You may find that you are offered a choice—take the low interest rate and pay a higher price for the car, or finance elsewhere and take a manufacturer's rebate. Often you will be much better off taking the rebate and financing at your local credit union.

We recognize that it's not always practical to pay cash for your purchases, especially major items like a house, car, college tuition, or even once-in-a-lifetime vacations. In those instances, avoid the first impulse of financing your purchase at the nearest bank or from the seller.

Look for funds from nontraditional sources. You may be pleasantly surprised at how you can structure your deal to everyone's benefit.

Take this example: You need a new car. Your clunker requires major repairs, is eight years old, and is literally on its last legs. But a new car will cost $12,000. The going rate is 12 percent, which means a $316 payment each month over four years or $399 a month over three years.

At the same time, a parent (or friend or relative) has that $12,000 sitting in a savings account earning a meager 7 percent. Retired parents often complain that they would like to earn more on their savings.

It's time to strike a deal, backed up by legal loan papers. Your parents (or others) lend you the $12,000 at 9.5 percent, splitting the difference between what you would have had to pay a bank and what the bank was paying on the savings. You'll pay less each month because of the lower interest rate; your parents will earn more because of the higher rate. You both win.

For a longer-term situation, you might want to use a different kind of setup. Say you want to buy a home. You may need to borrow the down payment from a relative. You may even be able to borrow the entire purchase price. Great. But now you're talking about a loan that could stretch out for fifteen years or more.

One alternative that works quite nicely is to do what the banks and other lenders do—tie the loan interest rate to some national rate like Treasury notes, the prime interest rate, or the going rate on a particular money market fund as of a certain date. Your private lender isn't earning that amount in savings. Also agree to adjust the rate once every six months or so. The strategy here is to avoid paying an excessively high mortgage loan interest rate while giving the lender more than she would get by leaving her money on deposit. You might agree to pay two percentage points over the savings rate offered by the bank, adjusted semiannually. That's fair.

Perhaps the very best source to look for borrowing is in your own home. We are great fans of home ownership, and even more so now that the 1986 Tax Reform Act is law. That's because the interest on your home mortgage is fully deductible, and consumer interest is being phased out as a deduction.

When you need a loan, consider tapping your home equity by either refinancing your present mortgage or taking out a second mortgage. Sometimes refinancing makes the most sense, especially when you are paying a hefty interest rate. Other times, applying for a home equity loan is the better deal. That way you can borrow only as much as you need, because, as with all loans, you have to repay it, plus interest. Either way, you will be using the funds to pay for something that you would ordinarily have to finance. You are trading nondeductible interest payments on a consumer loan for tax deductible interest payments on a mortgage loan. And that's smart.

There are other nontraditional sources you should consider when you must borrow.

You can take out a secured rather than an unsecured personal bank loan at a rate that is far below what credit card companies charge. Unsecured loans are too expensive. But when you can put up some collateral, the bankers drop the interest charges substantially.

If you own a whole life insurance policy, check its loan provisions based on its cash buildup. Often, you can borrow at rates as low as 5 percent.

Shop for rates. Frequently, one lender will offer significantly lower rates than others on one type of loan but higher rates on another.

Check out your credit union. If you don't belong to one, join. If one is not immediately available to you, try to join through a relative. Credit unions often charge lower interest rates on loans to their members because they are not profit-making operations.

# OCTOBER

## *Working for Yourself* and *How to Survive a Tax Audit*

Self-employment provides financial benefits from the day

you set up shop.

No one looks forward to a tax audit, but with the right

approach you have a good chance of coming out unscathed.

 *To Do*

- Monthly budget
- What business can you operate on the side out of your home? (see page 156)
- If you are interested in franchises, buy a copy of *The Franchise Annual Handbook and Directory* (see page 205)
- If you don't understand your company's pension plan, get literature from human resources. If you are retiring or retired, contact the companies you have worked for regarding your pension payments.

# *How to Be Your Own Boss*

Working for yourself could be the smartest move you'll ever make. Start small, part-time, and watch your business grow. The tax law argues for you to try it on your own, and so do all the success stories you read. Try it. You may like it.

Self-employment offers the greatest financial opportunity available today. Go to work for yourself. We both have, and we encourage others to try it. Now we are not telling you to march into your boss's office and announce you are quitting. That could be financial suicide. What we are suggesting is that you set up a small, at-home business on the side. If you're married, encourage your spouse to start his or her own enterprise, too. You'll work extra hours, but the financial and personal rewards are worth the effort.

Initially, you may ask what you could do to make any money. The response is limited only by your imagination. Start with your hobbies and other interests. If you are a decent photographer who is always being asked by family and friends to take shots of gatherings, start a full-fledged business.

Maybe you make wonderful pastries. There's always a market for parties. Or you like to entertain. You can handle the details for special occasions. Or you make superb flower arrangements. Sell them to boutiques. Or you tell stories. Hire yourself out to libraries and schools. Perhaps you swim. Establish a swim team and make some money by giving lessons. People like Famous Amos started small by baking the most wonderful cookies you ever tasted.

Start small, but don't be surprised if you make a success of it. After all, you have the firm's best interest at heart. No one will work harder for you than you will.

If you turn a hobby or interest into an operating business, you will transform what were previously your personal nondeductible expenses into legal tax deductions. Let's assume you are a photographer.

You own a couple of cameras and lenses. You've had your eye on another, more expensive camera but couldn't justify the price. The cost of film and developing is putting a crimp in the family budget.

So one day, after you get home from work, you decide to finally set up a sideline business as a professional photographer. Now you are an entrepreneur.

You open up a business checking account and register your business name with the appropriate authorities. You meet with an accountant to set up your books and get a business phone, business cards, and stationery. You advertise in the yellow pages and in the local paper. And you subscribe to various magazines that are used in the trade. All these expenses are tax-deductible.

You purchase the new camera plus two special lenses, which you will either depreciate or take as an expense. The film and developing costs are now tax-deductible.

You decide to attend a couple of regional trade shows. Again, all of your expenses can be offset against your income, as can your driving costs when you go to jobs. Review Lesson 39 on how to legitimately combine personal vacations with business trips and still write off the lion's share of the cost.

Your business may operate at a loss the first year or two, but that's OK. Although no one enjoys the idea of losing money, and you certainly have not entered into business to lose your shirt, your losses can be offset by the salary you earn at your regular job, plus your dividend and interest income. You do have to be profitable in three out of five consecutive years so the IRS cannot accuse you of operating a hobby rather than a full-fledged business. However, even if you are not as profitable as you should be, your business-like approach to your operation should carry the day.

You probably run your operation out of your home. Again, there are tax breaks available to you, primarily for utility and other upkeep expenses, along with depreciation on the house if your business is profitable. For a more thorough discussion, look at Lesson 37, "Tax Breaks of a Business at Home."

You have alternatives to going out on your own and starting a business. You might consider going into business with a friend or relative who has the same interests you have. Our advice to those who start a business with someone else is to visit a neutral attorney so legal papers can be drawn up protecting each partner's rights and interests just in case the business is not successful. It will pay in the long run to have all the details spelled out in advance. Some very successful people have started out by sharing an idea and have jointly carried through on it.

One example is the two mothers in our community who wanted to find appropriate camps for their children. They were diligent in their search, contacting dozens of camps. Friends and neighbors started asking them for advice for their own children. Over a period of only a few years, hundreds of camps have come to our area one weekend each winter to present their programs. The mothers now work as paid consultants for parents who want help selecting just the right camp for their youngsters. These women took a routine task and expanded it into a successful money-making business.

Another alternative is to buy into an existing enterprise. Your current employer may offer employees a share of the business for a cash investment. Or you may set up a competing business in the same field in which you presently work. Our travel agents, for example, toiled as employees for years. The owner of the agency decided to sell the operation, and they were the first potential buyers asked. They jumped at the chance. And today, they make a very nice income for themselves rather than for the ex-owner.

Or you may decide to go into a field that is already established, with lots of marketing and advertising help at your fingertips. Today, there are literally thousands of opportunities to work for yourself by buying into a nationally recognized franchise. If you have a cool quarter of a million dollars, you might be able to talk with McDonald's. An ice cream parlor franchise may cost you $100,000 or more. Don't let the money scare you; most of it is financed. Depending on the business that interests you, the amount of money you have available, and the number of hours you want to work, you may want to investigate the field of franchises. An excellent starting point is to visit your local library or bookstore for a copy of *The Franchise Annual Handbook and Directory*, published by Info Press, Inc. If the library or bookstore doesn't have it, write directly to 736 Center Street, Lewiston, New York 14092. This publication lists hundreds of franchise opportunities, whom to contact, and the amount of money it takes to get involved.

Whether you jump in with a franchise, work with a partner, buy out or compete with your present employer, or turn your hobby into an operating business, you will be working for yourself. Be prepared for success. What frequently happens after a year or two is that your business starts taking more of your time and starts generating more income. As with most endeavors, the more you put into it, the more benefits you reap. It may not be long before you will have an important decision to make—do you stay with your present job, or do you set out on your own? You're not starting from scratch. You've developed your own business over the past year or so and have both a growing client base and a cash flow. What starts out as a way to beat the tax collector often turns into a new way of life.

# *How to Survive a Tax Audit*

Surviving an audit is easy—when you are properly prepared for the confrontation with the Internal Revenue Service (IRS). Do your homework and you can walk away from your audit unscathed.

We won't try to kid you—audits are no fun. The IRS has enormous powers. It can empty your bank accounts, close your business, even sell your house if you have not been careful. Never ignore an IRS audit notice.

On the other hand, you needn't live in fear of being audited, assuming that you have honestly reported your income and accurately calculated your deductions and credits.

We've both been audited in the past few years, and we expect to be audited again. Neither of us has had to pay large tax deficiencies, penalties, or interest. We've both been well prepared for our audits because we understand the tax laws and we are good record keepers. Our example goes to prove the point that audits can be, for the most part, nothing more than minor irritations and inconveniences. Audits are something to get through as quickly as possible, without having to pay huge sums to the IRS.

Some people feel that the IRS only audits returns of people who have done something terribly wrong with their taxes; that honest, law-abiding taxpayers are never questioned. That's not true. We are not tax cheats, and we do not subscribe to doing anything the least bit shady. Yet we've been audited. The fact is that the tax law is terribly complicated. It's difficult for you—and at times, even for the IRS—to know exactly how to apply the law to today's financial dealings. Taxes are rarely black and white.

Every tax return sent in to the IRS is carefully scanned. Those that look out of the ordinary in some material respect are pulled for a closer review. Many of them result in letters or calls to taxpayers. "You're being audited. Come down with your papers so we can see proof of your deductions and credits, make sure that you interpreted the law and regulations correctly, and verify that you reported each bit of taxable income that's required."

To be on the safe side, anticipate that each tax return you file will be selected by the IRS for further questioning, even though a mere 1.2 percent of all returns filed are actually audited. That's not very many when you figure there are almost 100 million individual tax returns filed each year, to say nothing of corporate, partnership, employment, excise, estate and gift tax returns. Assuming there's nothing terribly unusual about your tax return, your chances of being audited are quite slim.

If you are a high-income taxpayer, someone earning more than $50,000 a year, your audit risk is approximately one in twenty. If you file the short form and earn under $10,000, your audit risk is well under one in a hundred. Your audit exposure varies, depending on your income level, investments in tax shelters, the size of your deductions, where you live and work, the kind of return you file (personal, business, employment, and so on), and even your occupation.

Before the IRS starts selecting returns for audit, it carefully checks each one for mathematical accuracy and to make sure you haven't made one or more of what it calls "obvious errors," like trying to deduct the Social Security taxes withheld from your pay or claiming one-half of a dependency exemption because you send funds to parents.

The IRS corrects math problems and obvious errors and adjusts your refund accordingly. If you owe more money, it sends a bill. You're not audited because of these problems.

In addition, each return is checked against the IRS's computer records for unreported income. If the IRS finds income that belongs to you but is not reported, out goes the letter asking you to pay tax on that sum. Again, this is not an audit. You may find that surprising. The IRS considers nonreporting of income by and of itself to be one of the most serious tax crimes you can commit. Yet when it matches a bit of unreported income with a return, it doesn't institute an audit but rather sends out a tax bill.

The actual selection of returns for audit takes place a year to eighteen months after you file. In the winter of 1986–87, the IRS was looking at 1984 returns that were filed by April 15, 1985.

OK, you know your audit risk is slight. But that doesn't make you feel any better when you receive that audit notice in the mail. To the IRS, this audit is not personal. Your audit is nothing more than an opportunity to prove to an IRS bureaucrat that what you put down on your tax return is correct and complete; and you can back up your claims with verifying records and receipts.

If you have those records, your auditor will walk away penniless. In fact, that happens in more instances than the IRS would like to admit. Approximately 15 to 20 percent of individual audits result in no change or even additional refunds being granted to the taxpayer. That just goes to prove that not everyone who is audited has to pay or has done something wrong.

Contrary to popular belief, auditors do not get a percentage of what they collect. And to the best of our knowledge and according to the IRS itself, auditors do not have production quotas. Auditors will not lose their job because of no-change audits. Their job is to determine the precise amount of tax due, no more and no less.

The key to winning your audit confrontation is preparation. Your auditor will be well prepared. The computer has reviewed your return and determined that there's a good chance something is amiss. That doesn't necessarily mean you've done anything wrong. It just means that, for example, some of your deductions may exceed what others in your income bracket are claiming. Those sections of your return that cause concern have been checked by an IRS tax-return classifier who has agreed with the computer's assessment of potential tax deficiency.

Your auditor will review your return, and will have prepared an audit plan. The areas that the auditor wants to check have been carefully laid out. You must be as fully prepared as your auditor. It's at this stage that the audit is won or lost.

We recommend that you spend whatever time is necessary to develop a complete preaudit strategy. If the return under examination was filled out by a professional preparer, you should contact that person. Remember, however, that some preparers will not act as your legal representative during the audit; you should always try to hire someone who will represent you. It is advisable for you to have a tax professional on your side during the audit, unless, of course, you have been audited before and are confident you can respond to every tax question.

The first step in your preaudit strategy session, whether you hold it alone or with a tax representative, is to respond to the audit notice. It will tell you to confirm your appointment or to set up a date that is more convenient. If you're hiring a representative, let him or her set the appointment at a convenient time and place for the two of you. Your auditor works regular business hours, so scheduling won't be a problem, although you will probably have to take some time off work.

Whoever calls to set up the appointment should find out two things—where the audit is to be held and how much time to allot for it. If the audit is to be held at IRS offices, chances are it will be a routine office audit and won't go into minute detail. If the audit is to be held outside IRS offices, it's your choice where to sit down and talk about your finances, as long as your records will be available. A good, neutral ground is your accountant's office.

Asking how long the audit should take will reveal further information. If the response is "only an hour or so," you know the auditor can't go into great depth. If, on the other hand, you are told to set out at least half a day and that the audit is likely to take four or five visits, you know that you're in for a real grilling. And there's not a thing you can do about it.

The next step is to carefully review the audit notice. It will usually specify precisely which areas of your return are of the most interest to your auditor. It may be that your tax and interest deductions, charity, investment gains and losses, or medical costs are out of line with the norms, and the auditor would like to see your records. You may have filed a Schedule C reporting your at-home business activities, and the auditor wants to see your books.

Compare the areas that the audit notice questions with the tax-return worksheets that you prepared when the return was filled out. In Lesson 11, we talked about the need for you to work out a detailed road map, setting forth precisely how you arrived at each number on your return. It may be from a canceled check or a compilation of charitable gifts. This worksheet can make your audit strategy session simple.

Next, it's time to organize those records, books, and receipts being questioned so you can quickly respond to the auditor's queries. Remember, the idea is to get in and out of the audit unscathed. Well-organized records are the only way to accomplish this. Any papers that are incomplete should be researched and reconstructed as accurately as possible. You may need to contact your mortgage company for a copy of its year-end statement if you misplaced yours. You might have to reconstruct your business driving expenses in order to nail down the full deduction for your car. Whatever is necessary as far as your record keeping is concerned, this is the time to do it.

Review your income, because the auditor will. It's standard procedure for the auditor to look through all your bank records, adding each deposit you made during the year and comparing that total with what you reported on your return. You must be able to explain any differences or be prepared to pay additional tax. Note the source of each deposit and whether or not it is taxable or tax-free. For example, you might have transferred $500 from your savings to your checking account. That shows up as an extra deposit, but it's not taxable. Or you may have taken out a bank loan. Bankers make you deposit loans before you can write a check on the funds. Loans aren't taxable either. Neither is the return of capital from the sale of investments, although the profits have to be reported.

At this point, you should be able to determine precisely how your audit is likely to turn out. You know whether or not you reported all your taxable income, and you know if you have records that will convince the auditor to allow your claimed deductions and credits. Your adviser can tell you if you will have trouble with interpretations of points of law, such as with deductions for office-in-your-home expenses.

You can take the fear of the unknown associated with your audit and reduce it to a precise number, or at least to a price range, by calculating the likely outcome of the audit. Based on your preaudit strategy sessions, you should know how much you might have to pay in back taxes if:

- The auditor locates every questionable item on your return that you can't absolutely verify. That rarely happens, simply because most auditors don't have the time or ability to dig through each and every nook and cranny in your return.
- The auditor denies the full amount of each item. Again, that's something that rarely happens because auditors understand the need for negotiation and compromise in order to close audits rather than having them drag on.
- The auditor's supervisors and superiors fully agree with the auditor's findings.

When you know the very worst the IRS can do to you as a result of an audit is deny, say, $3,000 in deductions, and that you are in the 38 percent tax bracket, you have reduced the fear of the unknown surrounding your audit to a maximum deficiency of $1,330, plus interest. If that's a number you can live with, you have nothing to worry about as the audit date approaches. If it's more than you can afford, then perhaps you could work harder to compile the records and receipts you'll need to make certain the worst-case scenario won't happen. If you just can't come up with the receipts you need, then resign yourself to your fate and vow to keep better records in the future.

You are as prepared as you can be. Sit back confidently and await your audit confrontation.

You should show up for your audit about fifteen minutes early. That will give you the opportunity to get acquainted with an impersonal federal office. It goes without saying that you need to have your records with you.

Once you meet the auditor, you may be pleasantly surprised to find that the confrontation usually begins on a cordial note. You might even exchange pleasantries. But don't be chatty. The auditor has a job to do. Get on with it. Auditors hate people who waste their time. Remember, each auditor may have twenty or more active cases on hand at any one time.

Respond only to questions that are directed to you. Your representative, if you have one, should field the technical queries. Don't argue politics. Don't get yourself labeled as a tax protester. Don't plead that everyone else takes a certain deduction so you should be able to, as well. Their time will come.

If the auditor switches gears and asks you something that you are not prepared to answer, be honest and say you're not ready, that the audit notice didn't cover that item, and that you will have to schedule another meeting to take care of it. It may be something that you can cover through the mail.

The auditor isn't going to hand you a bill when the audit session is over, because the procedure is not complete. He or she must write up an audit report and submit it to supervisors, who will either accept it or instruct the auditor to ask more questions and investigate more thoroughly. The audit is only complete when you receive a letter in the mail informing you that the audit report has been accepted.

# NOVEMBER

## *Saving for Retirement*

By combining Social Security, pensions from work, and IRAs, you can build a big retirement nest-egg—providing you tap every source and invest wisely.

 *To Do*

- Monthly budget
- Fourth and year-end tax review session (see page 48)
- Call for brochures on the mutual funds we recommend (see page 225; see also page 97)

# The Three-Legged Stool
## of Retirement Income

By taking advantage of tax incentives, you can build a prosperous retirement.

Traditionally, prudent Americans have built their retirement income on three legs—Social Security, a company pension, and an individual's own investments. That's still the way to do it, and even under the new tax law a large portion of your investments can be structured to avoid or delay income tax. There's nothing tricky or devious about these tax-saving devices. Congress wrote them into the law so Americans would provide for themselves in their old age, thus lessening dependence on the government.

First, let's kill a persistent myth. Doomsayers continue to warn that the Social Security system will collapse or that benefits will be drastically reduced. At the very least, these critics say, you'll get back much less than you paid in.

All this is nonsense. In fact, Social Security is the *only* major federal program that is securely financed for decades ahead, with no deficits in sight. In case you haven't noticed, your Social Security taxes—the FICA deduction from your paycheck—have been rising year by year. That's how Social Security works, with taxes from workers and their employers funding the pensions of retirees and other Social Security beneficiaries.

In 1986, workers making $42,000 or more paid Social Security taxes of $3,003, with their employers chipping in a like amount. If you retired in 1985 and had earned the top Social Security pension, you'd be getting $739 a month in 1986—a total of $8,868 for the year. Pensions rise every year in line with the previous year's inflation. Assuming your earnings qualify you for the top amount, you can look forward to an annual Social Security pension with the buying power of $8,868 in 1986 dollars.

If you're still dubious about Social Security, listen to this from

Robert J. Myers, whom we consider the nation's leading authority on Social Security. Myers is no dreamer; he was chief actuary of the Social Security Administration, then assistant commissioner, and later was executive director of the National Commission on Social Security Reform, which drew up the legislation, passed in 1983, that put the Social Security system on sound footing, way into the twenty-first century. Myers no longer works for the government, so he can speak freely, and he does:

> Despite what some people might believe, young people will get their money's worth—and somewhat more—from the Social Security taxes that they pay. . . . Not only is the Social Security program on a sound financial basis overall, but also it does provide people of all ages with at least a reasonably good buy of retirement-income protection.

Of course, $8,868 isn't nearly enough annual income. You'll need the other two legs of retirement support—company pensions and your own savings.

An astounding number of Americans have only a vague understanding of their company pensions. If you're one of those, stop by the personnel office and pick up enough printed material so you can figure out what you have to do to qualify for a pension and how much you can expect to collect. Typically, employees become vested—meaning entitled to benefits at age sixty-five—after five years of service. Under some plans, even less time is required.

That can be a significant factor in deciding when, or whether, to leave a job. It's downright foolish—or, in most cases, careless—to leave a job in October when you would become vested in November. That applies whether you're sixty years old or forty or twenty. We talk about "pensions" because most Americans work for several employers during their forty or so working years. By planning, you can earn a pension from most—maybe all—of your employers. Anytime you leave a job, make sure you know when and how you can start getting your pension. Keep in touch with your old employers; don't expect those companies to come looking for you on your sixty-fifth birthday. Apply for your pensions and make sure you get them.

The third leg of the retirement stool must be built from your own savings and investments, but the government has smoothed the road with wonderful tax incentives. The best known of these is the IRA, or Individual Retirement Account. News stories about the new tax law led many people to believe that the IRA is dead. Some people have asked us whether their existing IRA accounts will now be taxed. Here are three important facts about the IRA, as it stands now, *after* the new tax law:

First, your existing IRA accounts will not be taxed, and will continue to accumulate interest or dividends, free of federal income tax, until you withdraw the money, usually after age 59½.

Second, if you have not yet contributed to your IRA for 1986, you can do so until April 15, 1987. Just as before, you can contribute up to $2,000 of your 1986 wages, and your entire contribution will be deductible from your 1986 income tax. If your spouse earned $2,000 or more in 1986, he or she also can contribute—and deduct— the full $2,000. If one spouse worked and the other did not, the couple's IRA contribution can total $2,250. You can divide the $2,250 any way you like as long as neither account gets more than $2,000 or less than $250. Those were the rules for 1985 and they continue to apply for 1986. The limitations imposed by the new tax law apply to your IRA contributions for 1987 and beyond.

Finally, for 1987 and future years, $2,000 IRA tax deductions will continue to be fully available for about 75 percent of people who presently have IRAs. Another 15 percent will qualify for partial IRA deductions. Only about 10 percent will no longer be entitled to deduct an IRA contribution.

So the IRA is alive and kicking. Here are the new rules:

1. If neither you nor your spouse is covered by a company pension plan or a Keogh pension plan for the self-employed, both of you can continue to deduct a full $2,000 IRA contribution, just as before. No income ceiling applies.
2. If either you or your spouse is covered by a company pension plan or a Keogh plan, your IRA deduction will depend on your income. If you are single and your adjusted gross income is below $25,000, you are still entitled to take the full $2,000 IRA deduction. For every five dollars of adjusted gross income over $25,000, you lose one dollar of IRA deduction. So when your adjusted gross income hits $35,000 you can no longer deduct a penny of IRA contribution. If you are married and you and your spouse have adjusted gross income totaling less than $40,000, both of you can deduct a full $2,000 IRA contribution (assuming

you both earn that much during the year). Again, for every five dollars of adjusted gross income over $40,000 you both lose one dollar of IRA deductibility. So when your total adjusted gross income hits $50,000 neither of you can deduct a penny of IRA contribution.

(An important note: For this formula, you cannot count your IRA deduction in reaching your adjusted gross income figure. It's your adjusted gross income not counting any IRA deduction.)

3. Whether or not you are entitled to deduct an IRA contribution, you can continue to contribute to an IRA, and the dividends or interest will continue to accumulate tax-free until you withdraw the money, usually after age 59½. If you withdraw IRA money before age 59½, you must pay income tax on the withdrawal plus a penalty of 10 percent. So if you are not entitled to take a tax deduction for an IRA contribution, you should think hard about whether to contribute to your IRA. On the positive side, your contribution will accumulate interest or dividends free of income tax until you withdraw the money. On the negative side, if you withdraw money before age 59½ you get stuck with a penalty. On balance, it is very worthwhile to contribute if you will not need the money before age 59½, and if you cannot take care of your pension needs with more favorable plans.

In Lesson 51, we talk about where to invest your IRA money. Right now, let's talk about *when* to invest it. You can make your IRA contribution as early as January 1 or as late as April 15 of the following year—the tax-filing deadline. For your own sake, make that contribution early.

You don't believe it matters? Here's the difference. Let's say Lois makes her IRA contribution every January 1, while Fred doesn't make his until April 15 of the following year. Both contribute $2,000 a year, and both accounts earn 10 percent a year. The accompanying table shows the difference.

Many companies today offer their employees a tax-deferred pension savings program that is at least as good as an IRA. It's variously called a salary-reduction plan or a 401(k) plan, after the section of the Internal Revenue Code that describes it. A 401(k) is usually offered in addition to traditional company pension plans.

Under a 401(k), you sign up with your employer to have a portion of your pretax salary deferred and invested in the savings plan. Ten percent is typical; the new tax law limits your annual

## COMPARISON BETWEEN THE ACCUMULATED VALUE OF EARLY AND LATE IRA CONTRIBUTIONS

| End of year | $2,000 contributed on January 1 | $2,000 contributed 15½ months later, on April 15 | Difference at year's end |
|---|---|---|---|
| 1 | $ 2,200 | $ 0 | $ 2,200 |
| 5 | 13,431 | 9,757 | 3,674 |
| 10 | 35,062 | 28,548 | 6,514 |
| 15 | 69,899 | 58,871 | 11,088 |
| 20 | 126,005 | 107,551 | 18,454 |
| 25 | 216,363 | 186,046 | 30,317 |
| 30 | 361,887 | 312,464 | 49,423 |
| 35 | 596,254 | 516,062 | 80,193 |
| 40 | 973,703 | 843,957 | 129,746 |

contribution to $7,000. Many firms partially match the employee's contribution, and the new tax law does not limit the company's contribution. For example, you might elect to have 10 percent of your salary deducted for a 401(k), and for every dollar you save, your employer might add 50 cents.

All that money goes into a professionally managed retirement fund, and you pay no income tax on your contributions, or on the interest or dividends, until you withdraw money, usually after age 59½. Before age 59½, you can withdraw only your own contributions, and even then will have to pay income tax on the withdrawal plus a 10 percent penalty. The penalty is waived if you use the money to pay medical expenses that exceed 7.5 percent of your adjusted gross income.

If you work for yourself, full-time or part-time, you can take advantage of a Keogh retirement account—still another tax-sheltered investment. Effective in 1984, Congress made Keoghs more generous—and more complicated. The big tax law enacted in 1986 did not restrict Keoghs. If you qualify for a Keogh, the details are worth knowing.

There are now two kinds of Keoghs. The better one is called a "profit-sharing" Keogh. Every year, you can contribute $30,000 or 13.04 percent of your net self-employment income—whichever is *less*—to a profit-sharing Keogh. You pay no income tax on your contributions, or on the dividends or interest they earn, until you withdraw money. You can start withdrawals at age 59½. A profit-sharing Keogh is a generous and understandable plan. Take full advantage of it. Lesson 51 gives you tips on where to invest your Keogh money.

The second kind of Keogh is called a "money-purchase" plan. To a money-purchase Keogh, you can contribute $30,000 or 20 percent of net self-employment income, whichever is less. Your total Keogh contributions—to profit-sharing and money-purchase plans—can't exceed the $30,000/20 percent limit.

We don't like money-purchase Keoghs. The paperwork is much more complicated, and the plan is rigid, in contrast with the flexibility of profit-sharing Keoghs. With a profit-sharing Keogh, you can contribute one year, contribute a smaller percentage the following year, and contribute nothing at all the next year. As long as your contribution doesn't exceed the maximum, you can change it as often as you like. And you can start withdrawing money at age 59½ whether you're retired or still working.

Not so with a money-purchase Keogh. Whatever percentage of net self-employment income you contribute the first year, you must contribute nearly every year; few modifications are allowed. And you cannot withdraw money until you retire, no matter your age. Many self-employed people keep working, at least a little, until they are no longer able. As long as you report any self-employment income on your tax return, you're barred from tapping your money-purchase Keogh savings.

Our advice is this: Contribute the full 13.04 percent to a profit-sharing Keogh. If you want to go further, contribute 6.96 percent to a money-purchase Keogh. That gives you the maximum 20 percent contribution (and tax deduction). And it keeps the bulk of your Keogh savings in the more flexible plan.

Few self-employed people know it, but even after contributing right up to the Keogh limits, self-employed Americans can set up an additional Keogh, with an annual contribution limit of 10 percent of net self-employment income. You pay income tax on the money that you put into this Keogh, but not on the dividends or interest that it earns.


Younger Americans often ignore retirement savings, on the grounds that they can start saving later in life. We recommend, however, that you open an IRA or Keogh as soon as you begin your career. Even if you only contribute a few hundred dollars the first year, you'll be on your way. As the chart on page 219 shows, savings build most dramatically after a long period, because of the effects of compounding. So start early. You'll be glad you did.

# LESSON 51

## *Where to Invest Your IRA*

Invest your Individual Retirement Account (IRA) money for high
yield, and don't be casual about a percentage point of difference. By
the time you retire, one additional point of interest can amount to
$100,000 or more. If you want to seek faster growth, consider mutual
funds or REITs. Follow the same investment philosophy for other
tax-sheltered retirements accounts, such as 401(k)s and Keoghs.

An IRA cuts your taxes in two ways: your annual contribution is
deductible from your taxable income, assuming you qualify for the
deduction under the rules we describe in Lesson 50. Second, the
interest or dividends that it earns accumulate free of income tax.
 The deduction for your annual contribution is the same no matter
how you invest your IRA money. For example, if your tax bracket
is 28 percent, a $2,000 IRA contribution will cut your income tax
by $560. But your investment choice will greatly affect the second
benefit—the deferment of income tax on IRA interest or dividends.
And under the new tax law, you get this second benefit whether or
not you qualify for the deduction of your IRA contribution. (Although we talk about IRAs throughout this lesson, the same logic
applies to other tax-sheltered retirement savings programs, such
as 401(k) and Keogh accounts.)
 An IRA shelters interest, dividends and investment profits from
taxation, for as long as the money stays in your IRA. But an IRA,
for all its benefits, has drawbacks, too. If you lose money on an
IRA investment, you cannot deduct any of the loss. If you lose
money on an investment outside your IRA, you can deduct the entire loss against capital gains or—up to $3,000 a year—against or-
dinary income such as wages.
 Once you start withdrawing money from an IRA, usually at age
59½ or thereafter, you pay full income tax on every dollar withdrawn, regardless of the investment that produced it. To take a
very pessimistic example, let's say you actually lost money on your

IRA investments—that you contributed $20,000 over the years and that nest egg shrank to $15,000. Tough; you still have to pay full income tax on every dollar you withdraw.

So from a tax standpoint, the facts overwhelmingly favor conservative IRA investments in high-yielding certificates of deposit or bond mutual funds. In Lesson 27, we tell you how to find the best of these income-yielding investments. Please don't make the common mistake of buying CDs at your local bank without comparing yields available elsewhere. One additional percentage point of interest—just one point—can make a huge difference over the years.

People have trouble believing that $2,000 a year can ever amount to much, but it can. The accompanying table shows how much you'll accumulate, using three annual yields, if you invest $2,000 in an IRA every year.

As you can see, the growth of that IRA nest egg accelerates as the years pass. That's because of the magic of compound interest. The more you've saved and earned year by year, the more the nest egg will grow.

COMPARISON BETWEEN THE ACCUMULATED VALUE OF IRA
CONTRIBUTIONS AT THREE ANNUAL YIELDS

|  | Total investment | Annual yield | | |
|---|---|---|---|---|
|  |  | 6% | 12% | 15% |
| After 15 years | $30,000 | $ 49,345 | $ 83,507 | $109,345 |
| After 25 years | 50,000 | 116,313 | 298,668 | 489,424 |

The tax laws point you toward an income-yielding IRA program. But is that also the best investment? Given the historical fact that stocks yield more over the long term than bonds or CDs, should you put your IRA money in one of the growth stock funds that we recommend in Lesson 21? After all, growth stock funds are tailor-made for long-term investing, and an IRA is surely a long-term investment.

The answer depends on your age, your investments outside your IRA, and your disposition. We believe in a balanced investment program (see Lesson 26). If you can save more than $2,000 a year, use your IRA for high-yield investments and invest outside your IRA in a growth mutual fund. If you can barely scrape up $2,000 a year and want to go for more rapid growth than you could get from bonds or CDs, strike a compromise: put your IRA savings in a growth-and-income mutual fund (Lesson 21) or a real estate investment trust (Lesson 33). These investments pay good dividends and also offer prospects for growth.

You can mix all these approaches, because you can open as many IRA accounts as you want, as long as you never contribute more than $2,000, in total, any year. The older you get, the more you should lean toward conservative, high-yield investments. The younger you are, the more you might consider growth-oriented investments. In later years, you can switch your IRA money to a bond fund or some other high-yield haven.

It's easy to switch IRA money from one account to another by mail or wire. The transfer is made automatically. Once a year you're allowed a different kind of transfer, called a "rollover." You simply close one IRA account, get the money, and put it in another IRA account. You're allowed to keep the money for sixty days in between, so you can use your IRA to provide an interest-free loan. But don't dally. If you keep the money even one day beyond the sixty-day limit, you have to pay income tax on the withdrawal and pay a 10 percent penalty, too.

The IRA contribution limits are $2,000 for an individual, $2,250 for a couple if only one spouse works. That $2,250 must be divided between two accounts; you can divvy it any way you want as long as neither account gets more than $2,000 of the $2,250.

That so-called spousal IRA is available only when the nonworking spouse earns less than $250. On the other hand, the $2,000 contribution allowed for any worker, or alimony recipient, can be the first $2,000 that comes in. If you work just enough to earn $2,000 in the year, you can put every penny of it in your IRA. Nor does the dollar that you put in your IRA have to be the same greenback that you earn. You can put $2,000 into your IRA on January 1, even if your only paycheck for the year doesn't arrive until the following December. See Lesson 51 for restrictions on IRA deductions mandated by the new tax law.

A $2,000 IRA contribution is a lot better than a $250 spousal contribution. If you are self-employed, full-time or part-time, and your spouse doesn't have a job, consider hiring him or her enough to earn $2,000 a year. The $2,000 you pay your spouse is deductible from your self-employment income. Your spouse has to report that

$2,000 as income—but then deducts it further down the tax form as an IRA contribution, assuming the two of you qualify for an IRA deduction under the 1986 tax law.

You want us to make it really easy for you? OK, here are three sample IRA portfolios:

First, for the very conservative investor, the investor who is approaching age 59½ and will soon be withdrawing IRA money, or the investor who is building a healthy nest egg of growth mutual funds outside an IRA: $1,500 in a high-yield CD or a short-term bond fund such as Fidelity Thrift Trust ([800] 544-6666) or Vanguard Fixed Income Short Term Bonds ([800] 523-7025); $500 in a money market mutual fund or an insured money market account.

Next, for the investor who wants to mix yield with growth: $2,000 in Evergreen Total Return Fund ([800] 635-0003), Fidelity Equity Income Fund ([800] 544-6666), or a blue-chip real estate investment trust (REIT) such as Federal Realty or United Dominion Realty. You have to buy REITs through a broker. See Lesson 33.

Last, for the venturesome investor who wants to seek high growth without risking the entire IRA nest egg: $1,000 in Twentieth Century Select Fund ([816] 531-5575) or Weingarten Equity ([212] 557-8787); $1,000 in a high-yield CD or a short-term bond fund.

Don't worry about building up so much IRA money that you'll never be able to spend it. IRA money is added to your estate and is passed to your heirs, subject to the usual estate tax.

# LESSON 52

## *A Delicious Choice Called "Lump-Sum Distribution"*

When you quit your job or retire, you may get your pension in one lump sum. What you do with it could save you thousands of dollars in taxes.

Many workers today are granted one of life's nicest choices—what to do with a lump-sum pension distribution. It comes about when you change jobs or retire and the company gives you your vested interest in the firm's pension or profit-sharing plan. If you have participated in a 401(k) pension plan, you'll get that nest egg when you leave your company.

These lump sums can amount to six-figure nest eggs, and the federal income tax law lets you choose either of two ways to avoid or minimize taxes. Both are generous. You have sixty days to decide; your company will provide the appropriate forms.

*Choice 1:* You can roll the money into a separate Individual Retirement Account, paying no income tax on the funds until they are withdrawn—usually at retirement, when your tax bracket is lower than during your working years.

*Choice 2:* You can take the money and invest (or spend) it as you please, paying a special reduced tax with a device called "five-year forward averaging." You pay tax on the lump sum as though you had received it in equal installments over five years and as if that were your only income for those five years, ignoring your salary and other income. If you are 50 or older, you figure on the basis of ten years instead of five.

With choice 1, you pay no tax now but will have to pay tax later as you withdraw the money from your IRA.

With choice 2, you pay tax now but not later, and the rate at which you pay now is very favorable. Moreover, you can use the money now rather than waiting until you are 59½. You might want to buy a vacation home or take a sabbatical. The lump sum might arrive in time to pay for your children's education.

If you considered your lump sum primarily as a nest egg to pass on to your heirs, you might be better off with choice 1. You could roll the money into an IRA and withdraw as little as the law allows, leaving the rest to your spouse or other heirs. Although the law permits IRA withdrawals starting at age 59½, it does not require you to withdraw money from your IRA until you are 70½.

The 1986 tax law reduced the advantages of choice 2. Previously, you could forward average for ten years; the new law cut it to five years except for people 50 or older. Moreover, the lower tax rates that will go into effect in 1987 and 1988 affect your choice. This is the kind of problem we all hope to face. A lump-sum distribution is a bonanza, and both of the two alternatives are very favorable.

# LESSON 53

## *A Word about Wills*

You'll need a lawyer to draw up a will. But you don't need an outsider to take a step that may be almost as important—open discussion within the family about who will inherit what.

Inheritance is a forbidden subject in many families. Most prudent Americans draw up wills, but few of them tell their future heirs what to expect. Children and other beneficiaries are loath to ask, for obvious reasons.

However understandable it may be, this silence partially defeats the purpose of a bequest. If you love your children enough to leave them your estate, you should love them enough to tell them how much to expect. If your own parents are elderly, you shouldn't feel guilty if you wonder how much they're willing to you. That's human nature; it doesn't mean that you're looking forward to their deaths.

That may sound callous. But authorities agree that knowledge is an important part of the American tradition of passing wealth from one generation to the next. Most "children" who inherit from their parents are in fact middle-aged people planning their own futures. They may be considering changing careers, retiring early, or buying a second home. They can take much better stock of their financial position if they know whether they're in line to inherit property from their parents and approximately how much.

For the same reasons, it's important to tell your children if you don't have much to leave or if you're leaving it to someone else—for example, a charity.

Don't assume that this is a problem reserved to the rich. Inheritances of $100,000 or more are common these days, largely because so many older Americans own their own homes and real estate values have risen so much during the past decade or two. With estate taxes declining, it's not at all unusual for heirs to find themselves dividing an estate totaling several hundred thousand dollars, from parents who had been considered people of relatively modest means.

Robert A. Stein, dean of the University of Minnesota Law School, is one of the nation's leading authorities on probate (estate) law. Stein understands the human side of estate law, too. Face it, he advises: your heirs are going to discuss your will eventually. Adds Stein: "I'd much rather have that discussion go on when I'm there and can participate in it." Amen.

# DECEMBER

## *Staying "Rich"*

After you retire, many of the investment strategies you've followed to build a nest-egg suddenly work best in reverse. Keep this in mind if you are still working. Adapt our program for the next year and maintain your commitment to your finances.

 *To Do*

- Monthly budget
- If you have a family, discuss your will openly
- Review the status of your investments
  - If you are retired or are nearing retirement, consider investment changes you will make when you stop working (see page 233)
- Invest to maximize dollar-cost averaging (see page 100)
- Start your tax folder for the next year
- Set up your calendar for the next year. Mark all fixed tax dates in bold

- Set personal finance goals for the next year. Plan to follow up on ideas you were unable to implement this year, and assign them to specific months

## *How to Stay "Rich," Even after Retirement*

Once you retire, you need to take a step back and dispassionately analyze your finances. That includes your monthly budget, net worth, investments, insurance, taxes, and the various other topics we've discussed in this book. Many of the financial premises you've lived by during your working career need to be reexamined, and changed where appropriate. Instead of growth, you may want income. Instead of tax-exempts, you may want taxable corporate bonds.

If you are retired, you need to work diligently to keep what you have saved and invested. If you are still working, you should remember that one day you will join the ranks of the retired.

That's why it is important for both the retiree and the not-yet-retired person to keep the information in this lesson in mind.

Throughout your working career, you should have planned for the time you would retire. Hopefully, the financial portion of your game plan involved watching your nest egg grow without having the Internal Revenue Service (IRS) take a hefty bite. Chances are you put your money into growth securities; the IRS doesn't tax growth until the asset is sold. Or you invested in tax-exempt bond mutual funds, so the IRS wouldn't tax your interest income. Perhaps you were able to do better after taxes with a tax-exempt bond paying 7 percent than with a fully taxed bond paying 9 percent. You purchased life insurance to protect your family in case of your untimely death. You also covered the possibility of temporary incapacity by owning disability insurance to replace lost income. You invested in Individual Retirement Account (IRA) and Keogh retirement plans. The contributions were tax-deductible, cutting your income tax. The interest, dividends, and growth accumulated tax-deferred until withdrawn sometime after you reach age 59½. Perhaps you own rental real estate.

When you retire from the active work force, you must change much of the financial thinking you employed while working. For example, there is no reason for you to pay premiums on disability insurance when you're retired. Save your money.

Consider your life insurance needs, too. The purpose of the insurance is to take care of those you leave behind. If many of those people, particularly your adult children, are now financially self-sufficient, the need for much of your life insurance has ended. Quit paying the premiums on insurance you don't need. If you only have your spouse to care for in the event of your untimely death, carry just the amount of insurance needed to make sure he or she is comfortable. Drop the extra insurance coverage and withdraw any cash still in the policy.

We know one retired husband who insists on maintaining the sizable whole life policy he has paid on for years. He's now seventy, and his wife is convinced that as soon as he stops paying the premium, he's going to die. No one can convince her of the folly of this line of thinking.

If you have term insurance, save the premium. If you have been paying on whole life, you will have built up a nest egg that can either be cashed in or used to generate annuity income, depending on the terms of your policy and your age.

Carefully review the status of your IRA and Keogh retirement accounts. Once you're past the age of 59½, all withdrawals are fully taxed. Take that into account as you tap your retirement accounts. Withdraw only what you need. There is a minimum-withdrawal provision when you reach the age of 70½. Contact your retirement account custodian for a detailed withdrawal schedule.

Also review the status of your account in your ex-employer's pension program. Determine the amounts you can count on receiving month in and month out, whether you can withdraw a lump sum and reinvest it yourself, and whether you can elect a survivor annuity for your spouse.

Another way of thinking that has to change concerns tax-exempts. When tax brackets were as high as 50 percent, it made sense to buy tax-exempt municipal bonds paying 7 percent when banks were only paying 9 percent on long-term certificates of deposit (CDs). To come up with an equivalent yield, the banks would have had to pay 16 percent on their CDs. That's all changed now that personal tax rates are lower.

When you retire and your taxable income is lower, you may be better off with high-yielding taxable investments rather than tax-exempt bonds. To help you make the choice, see Lesson 27.

You should also review your investments when you retire. Many people hold on to outdated investment philosophies, ones that worked fine during their high-income years but that are inappropriate during retirement. People get emotionally attached to securities they've owned for years, refusing to sell when they should.

You may have owned a favorite stock for years. It's increased in value year after year but paid almost nothing in dividends. That's fine while you're working and have a steady source of income. Then you don't want more taxable income as your goal is capital appreciation. But in retirement, you'll want to forgo the growth and tap into the income. It may be time to sell the growth stock and switch the proceeds into an income mutual fund.

You'll want to keep track of your Social Security benefits, especially when you are under the age of seventy. Under current law, those receiving Social Security benefits while still working will find their benefits reduced by $1 for each $2 of earned wages, once they earn more than certain levels. These are adjusted annually to reflect increases in inflation. For 1986, those under the age of sixty-five could earn up to $5,760 before benefits were reduced. Those sixty-five to sixty-nine could earn $7,800. Those seventy and older do not have their Social Security benefits cut by outside earnings.

Up to half of your monthly Social Security benefits may now be subject to income tax. You need to take that into consideration as you make your financial plans during retirement. The amount of income tax depends entirely on the level of your other income, including any tax-exempt income you might receive. Currently, single taxpayers with more than $25,000 in income will have half their Social Security taxed. The tax reaches married couples with more than $32,000 in income.

If you find that your retirement finances are getting a bit shaky or that you're getting bored and would enjoy returning to work, go ahead. There's nothing quite like staying active. It's a terrific way to supplement your retirement needs, even if you lose a portion of your Social Security benefits.

But let's end two misconceptions about age and taxes. No matter what your age, if you have taxable income, you are required to file a tax return. And if you are salaried or earn more than $400 in net self-employment income, you must pay Social Security taxes.

That's true even though you may be receiving Social Security benefits.

In retirement, you often have more time to plan your financial affairs than when you were working. Stay on top of things. After all, it's your money.

You also have the chance to be more creative than in the past. You might want to dump that rental property. After all, the tax breaks aren't going to do you much good if you are in a lower tax bracket.

Or if you own your home but need additional income, why not sell it to your son or daughter, taking back a private mortgage? You pay your kid 80 percent of the fair market rent. That's what the courts have allowed when there is a very trustworthy tenant. Then your kid pays you interest on the mortgage.

## *Sticking with It*

Money management is not something you do once and then forget. If you stick with the lessons in this book, your nest egg will grow and you will move rapidly toward meeting your financial goals.

We've given you a month-by-month system of money management. Don't throw it away with the old calendar.

Keep it up to date. Schedule five tax-planning sessions every year, not just the first year. Review your investments twice this year and twice next year and twice the year after.

It won't take much time. In fact, our system is designed to *save* time. We haven't loaded you down with a lot of research or paperwork or tedious reading. And the more familiar you get with money management, the easier it will become.

But stick with it. Make it part of your monthly routine. You'll be glad you did. Follow up on any ideas you weren't able to implement on your first reading. Our system doesn't take much time the second time through, because you no longer have to learn from the ground up. But it pays off more and more each year, as you become more adept at managing your money. So don't neglect our system—or your money.

# Glossary

*Adjusted gross income*—All your income from taxable sources, minus several specific "adjustments," which amount to deductions. They're listed at the bottom of the first page of Federal tax Form 1040.

*Audit*—A review of your tax return by the Internal Revenue Service.

*Basis*—Your cost, used in figuring gain or loss, when you sell a house or other property, such as stocks, bonds, or mutual funds. On real estate, basis includes the price you paid plus the cost of improvements.

*Basis point*—One one-hundredth of one percent. A term used to express day-to-day changes in the yield of bonds, based on market values.

*Bear*—Someone who expects stock prices to decline.

*Bear market*—A period when stock prices are declining.

*Beneficiary*—A person who receives the benefits of an insurance policy. If you buy a life insurance policy and set it up so your spouse will get the proceeds at your death, your spouse is the beneficiary.

*Bond*—An IOU issued by a federal, state, or local government agency or by a corporation. When you buy a bond, you are lending money to the agency or corporation. The agency or corporation promises to pay you a set percentage of interest every year and to repay your money—the principal—when the bond matures. To use investment jargon, a bond is a fixed-income investment.

*Bond mutual fund*—A mutual fund that buys a variety of bonds and pays the interest to shareholders.

*Broker*—A salesperson who makes his or her living by charging a commission on every transaction.

*Bull*—Someone who expects stock prices to rise.

*Bull market*—A period when stock prices are rising.

*Call*—See *Option*.

*Capital gain or loss*—Profit or loss on the sale of real estate, mutual funds, or anything else of value. Prior to the 1986 tax law, long-term capital gains were taxed at a more favorable rate than other income. That is no longer true.

*Capital gains distribution*—Money distributed to mutual fund shareholders, representing the fund's capital gains.

*Casualty loss*—A loss resulting from a sudden or unusual event, such as lightning's destroying your prize magnolia tree or a thief's making off with the family jewels. A casualty loss is tax-deductible to the extent that you do not collect insurance and the loss exceeds 10 percent of your adjusted gross income.

*Certificate of deposit (CD)*—A deposit in a bank or savings institution for a specified period of time, paying a specified rate of interest.

*Commission*—The fee a broker collects from buying or selling something for you, whether it be a house or shares of stock.

*Common stock*—A unit of ownership of a corporation. Some corporations also issue preferred stock. Holders of preferred stock get first call on any money available for dividends. Common stock carries more risk than preferred stock but also offers more opportunity for gain, or profit.

*Corporate bond*—A bond issued by a corporation.

*Coverage*—A term used in insurance to describe the amount of your protection. For example, if your life insurance coverage is $100,000, your beneficiary will get $100,000 when you die.

*Credits*—Dollar-for-dollar subtractions from the income tax you otherwise would pay. For example, the credit for child and dependent care expenses. Tax credits are more valuable than tax deductions, but tax deductions are more plentiful.

*Deductions*—Expenses subtracted from your adjusted gross income. For example, real estate taxes and interest on your mortgage.

*Deficiency*—Additional income tax that you owe.

*Depreciation*—A tax deduction reflecting the gradual wearing out of a business asset, such as a sales rep's car or a house that you own and rent out.

*Dividend*—Money paid by a corporation to its shareholders—the owners of its stock.

*Dollar-cost averaging*—A system of regularly investing a set amount—for example, $500 every three months. Dollar-cost averaging evens out swings in the stock market, reducing the investor's risk.

*Dow Jones Industrial Average*—A statistical barometer of the stock market, reflecting day-to-day price changes in the stocks of thirty large companies. Often called "the Dow" for short.

*Earned income*—Money you earn from working, as opposed to unearned income from interest and dividends.

*Earnings*—Profits, as in "XYZ Company reported earnings of 35 cents a share."

*Equity*—Stock. An "equity investor" is someone who buys stocks.

*Equity mutual fund*—A mutual fund that buys stocks, as opposed to a fund that buys bonds or other kinds of securities.

*Estimated tax*—The income tax that you anticipate paying for the current year.

*Exemption*—On your federal income tax form, an exemption represents someone you support, including yourself. If you live with your spouse and two children, you have four exemptions. Each exemption cuts your taxable income by $1,080 for 1986, $1,900 for 1987, $1,950 for 1988, and $2,000 for 1989 and afterwards.

*Filing status*—On your federal income tax form, your filing status determines the tax rate schedule that you use. The most common are "single" and "married, filing joint return."

*Futures contract (futures, for short)*—Buying an asset today for delivery in the future. In effect, an investment, or bet, based on the future price of the asset. Risky.

*Ginnie Mae (GNMA)*—Government National Mortgage Association. A U.S. government agency that guarantees certain mortgage securities.

*Gross income*—All your income from taxable sources. After calculating your gross income on your tax return, you can take off adjustments, then deductions, and finally exemptions.

*Growth stock*—A stock that seems likely to improve in value, or "grow." The term is usually applied to stocks with a history of growth. A growth mutual fund is a fund that concentrates on growth stocks.

*Holding period*—The length of time you own a piece of property, such as a house, or shares of a mutual fund.

*Income averaging*—A tax-saving device that let you average income over the previous four years, lessening the tax that you otherwise would pay if one year's income took a big jump. You can use Income Averaging on your 1986 taxes, but never again; it was killed by the new tax law.

*Individual Retirement Account (IRA)*—A tax-favored method of saving money toward retirement.

*Interest*—Payments a borrower makes to a lender for the use of money. A bank pays you interest on your deposits; a corporation or government agency pays you interest on bonds; you pay interest on your mortgage and other debts.

*Interest rate*—The interest payable each year, expressed as a percentage of the principal.

*Itemized deductions*—Deductions from your taxable income, listed on Schedule A, Form 1040.

*Keogh account*—A tax-favored retirement savings plan for the self-employed. Much like an Individual Retirement Account (IRA), but more generous.

*Leverage*—The use of borrowed money to invest. Risky.

*Liabilities*—Debts and other financial obligations.

*Liability*—Your obligation to pay for injury or damage legally caused by you—for example, in an auto wreck. Liability insurance protects you against this kind of risk.

*Liquid*—Easy to sell. Mutual fund shares are liquid, because you can sell them immediately by making a phone call. A house is less liquid because it takes time to sell it.

*Load*—Sales commission. A load mutual fund is one that charges a sales commission when you buy. A no-load fund is one that charges no sales commission.

*Maturity*—The date on which you get your principal back from a bond. If you buy a twenty-year bond on March 1, 1987, its maturity date will be February 28, 2007.

*Mortgage*—A loan with real estate as collateral. When you take out a mortgage to buy a house, you are borrowing money; if you fail to keep up the payments, the lender can seize the house.

*Mortgage securities*—Securities backed by mortgage loans. A bunch of individual mortgages are bundled together and sold to investors in the form of mortgage securities. A Ginnie Mae is a mortgage security.

*Municipal bond*—A bond issued by a state or municipality. Interest paid on general purpose municipal bonds is exempt from federal income tax.

*Mutual fund*—A portfolio of investments, managed by a professional, in which the public is invited to invest.

*NASDAQ*—National Association of Securities Dealers Automated Quotations. A market on which many stocks are traded. In general, stocks of large companies are listed on the New York Stock Exchange, while stocks of smaller corporations are listed on NASDAQ or on the American Stock Exchange.

*New York Stock Exchange*—Far and away the largest trading center, or market, for stocks. Also called the NYSE or the Big Board.

*Option*—A right to buy or sell a fixed number of shares of a certain stock at a specified price within a limited period of time. A "call" is a right to buy; a "put" is a right to sell. Options are high-risk investments sold through brokers.

*Penalty*—Additional money you're assessed by the Internal Revenue Service (IRS) for filing your tax return late or failing to pay enough estimated income tax or breaking other IRS rules.

*Point*—A word with different definitions for different investments. When a stock goes up a point, it goes up $1. When a bond goes up a point, it goes up $10. When the Dow Jones Industrial Average goes up a point, it rises from, say, 1,750 to 1,751, with no percentage implied. When you take out a mortgage, a point is 1 percent of the mortgage loan, paid up front.

*Portfolio*—A holding of securities. Your portfolio might consist of three hundred shares of one mutual fund and two hundred shares of another, plus $5,000 in a money market fund. A mutual fund's portfolio might consist of stocks in a hundred companies, plus assorted bonds and cash.

*Preferred stock*—Stock that has first call on any money to be paid out in dividends.

*Price-earnings ratio*—Market price per share divided by net earnings per share in the preceding year. A gauge of whether a stock is priced too low, too high, or about right.

*Principal*—The capital value of an investment, as opposed to the interest or dividends that it pays. Also the amount of a debt, as opposed to the interest paid on the debt.

*Principal residence*—The home you live in the majority of the time, as opposed to a vacation home or a home you rent out.

*Prospectus*—A booklet, required by law, that describes a security, such as a mutual fund.

*Put*—See *Option*.

*Redeem*—Cash in. When you redeem shares of a mutual fund, you exchange them for their current market value, in cash.

*REIT*—Real estate investment trust. A company that owns and rents out commercial real estate. A REIT issues stock and pays dividends.

*Rollover*—The reinvestment of the proceeds from one security into another of the same kind. When a certificate of deposit (CD) matures, you can take the cash or take a rollover into another CD. You can use a rollover to switch from one mutual fund to another.

*SEC*—Securities and Exchange Commission. The federal agency that regulates the securities business.

*Securities*—Stocks, bonds, mutual funds, and other investments for which you get a piece of paper to signify your ownership.

*Taxable income*—Your income after taking off adjustments, deductions, and exemptions.

*Tax-exempt bond*—See *Municipal bond*.

*Treasury bond*—A bond issued by the U.S. Treasury. The safest kind of bond, because the U.S. government pledges to pay it off, come what may.

*Unearned income*—Income from sources other than work, such as interest and dividends.

*Warrant*—A security issued by a corporation, giving the warrant holder the right to buy stock in the corporation at a stipulated price, within a set time period. In effect, a bet that the stock will rise in value before the warrant expires. Risky.

*Wash sale*—The sale of a stock or bond at a loss and the repurchase of an essentially identical stock or bond within thirty days.

*Withholding*—Money your employer takes out of your paycheck and turns over to Uncle Sam. Through withholding, you pay income tax on your salary gradually, all year long.

*Yield*—Dividend and/or interest payments on a stock, bond, mutual fund, or other security.

# Index

1 2 3 4 5 6 7 8 9 10 11 12 13 14 15 16 17 18

## JULY: *Affording College* and *Tax Deductible Vacations*

- Make plans to meet your children's education expenses (see page 163).
- Buy "Don't Miss Out: The Ambitious Student's Guide to Financial Aid" (see page 170).
- Plan business trips to take advantage of tax deductible vacations (see page 172).
- Have you funded your retirement account for the current year?

19 20 21 22 23 24 25 26 27 28 29 30 31

1 2 3 4 5 6 7 8 9

## AUGUST: *Insu*

- **August 15: Tax extension.**
- Review all insuran
- Order free copy o Organization "Buy 185).
- Call Insurance Inf insurance rates arc
- Buy mutual fund is gust/early Septemb

19 20 21 22 23

1 2 3 4 5 6 7 8 9 10 11 12 13 14 15 16 17 18

## OCTOBER: *Working for Yourself* and *How to Survive a Tax Audit*

- What business can you operate on the side out of your home? (see page 136).
  - If you are interested in franchises, buy a copy of *The Franchise Annual Handbook and Directory* (see page 205).

19 20 21 22 23 24 25 26 27 28 29 30 31

1 2 3 4 5 6 7 8 9

## NOVEMBER:

- Evaluate your reti
- If you don't unde plan, get literatur are retiring or ret worked for regard
- Take advantage o plan offered by yo
- Have you funded y
- Year-end tax revie
- Call for brochures mend (see pages 9

19 20 21 22 23

10 11 12 13 14 15 16 17 18

*ance*

return due if you filed for

e needs.

National Insurance Commerce
er's Guide" booklet (see page

rmation and check out the best
und the country (see page 179).
ue of Forbes Magazine (late Au-
er).

4  25  26  27  28  29  30  31

---

1 2 3 4 5 6 7 8 9 10 11 12 13 14 15 16 17 18

## SEPTEMBER: *Borrowing Wisely*

- **September 15: Third estimated tax payment due.**
- Tax review session, early September (see page 48).
- Call BankCard Holders of America for best credit card rates (see page 194).
- If you need to borrow money, check alternative sources.
- Consider joining a credit union.

19  20  21  22  23  24  25  26  27  28  29  30

---

10 11 12 13 14 15 16 17 18

*aving for Retirement*

ement needs, if appropriate.
rstand your company's pension
from Human Resources. If you
red, contact companies you have
ng pension payments.

any 401(k) retirement savings
r employer (see page 218).
ur IRA for the current year?
v session (see page 48).
on the mutual funds we recom-
–98).

24  25  26  27  28  29  30

---

1 2 3 4 5 6 7 8 9 10 11 12 13 14 15 16 17 18

## DECEMBER: *Staying "Rich"*

- Year-end investment review.
  - If you are retired or nearing retirement, consider investment changes to make when you stop working (see Lesson 54).
- Start tax folder for next year.
- Set up calendar for next year. Mark all fixed tax dates in bold.
- Set personal finance goals for next year. Assign specific months to follow up on ideas you were unable to implement this year.

19  20  21  22  23  24  25  26  27  28  29  30  31